ED Ⱶ

MOUNTAIN — CLIMBING — MONEY

A Kingdom guide to investing and aligning your money with Heaven

Mountain Climbing Money

Business name: Harris Advisors LLC
Address: 39555 Orchard Hill Place, Suite 600 Novi, MI 48375
Website: www.harrisadvisorsonline.com

ISBN 978-0-9966744-7-8

DEDICATION

To Ricky, Mom and Dad. God used your sacrifice as fuel for my fire in His service.

CONTENTS

FOREWORD

By LANCE WALLNAU

It's been over a decade since I began teaching on the seven mountains of cultural formation—the idea (introduced in the '70s by Loren Cunningham, Bill Bright, and Francis Schaeffer) that culture is shaped through seven primary areas of influence: family, religion, education, media, arts/entertainment, government, and business. Lasting change in culture only comes when all of these areas are practically and ideologically impacted. Since that time, I have been calling and equipping believers to fulfill Christ's mandate to disciple the nations by positioning themselves strategically within these mountains.

Contrary to what many assume, the "top of the mountain" is not the only or even most important position for believers in society. Rather, as Jesus' metaphors of salt, light, and leaven indicate, kingdom influence flows to society through believers who are unobtrusively scattered throughout the whole, bringing out the "God flavors... [and] God-colors in the world" (Matthew 5:13-14 MSG). The real work of discipling nations is not taking place in the four walls of a church building; rather, is unfolding as small groups of believers—what I call "micro churches"—band together, as Daniel and his three friends did in the courts of Babylon, to demonstrate the wisdom, truth, and love of the kingdom in whatever field, meeting, opportunity, project, team, or venture to which God assigns them.

In order for these micro-churches to be effective in discipling, believers must themselves be discipled. That is, they must master the kingdom disciplines that give them the thinking, behavior, character, and wisdom that set them apart and make them capable of bringing true influence to the world around them. Among these disciplines, one in which many believers remain untrained is the area of managing financial resources with kingdom wisdom for kingdom purpose. Believers are called to send a message to the world about what money is actually for, but many of them don't even know what that message is, much less how their use of money is out of sync with it.

I've known Ed Harris since he was a young man just starting out in his calling nearly twenty years ago. Ed was an early adopter of the seven mountains message, and I have eagerly watched his journey to climb his own mountain and gain unique mastery as a teacher and financial advisor. This book is a beautiful marriage of Ed's insightful teaching on kingdom purpose and his practical wisdom for aligning your financial resources with that purpose. Ed has a gift for connecting with the hearts of believers who long to participate in Christ's mission and mandate in the earth, yet continuously find themselves struggling against a deficit, whether of resources, wisdom, or purpose. If that is you, get ready to gain the tools, insight, and inspiration to overcome those deficits in the pages ahead. Now is the time for you to to take your place on your mountain.

Dr. Lance Wallnau
President: Lance Learning Group
Dallas, Texas
www.Lancewallnau.com

— PART 1 —

MOUNTAIN CLIMBING MONEY

A movement of cultural activism is sweeping our country and the world. Computer hackers are doing it. Hedge funds are doing it. Entrepreneurs and politicians are doing it. The twenty-somethings are serious about doing it. This growing movement is causing people to focus on more than making money or providing for a certain lifestyle. Instead of focusing on making ends meet or achieving a level of success according to the standards of society, many people are now focusing on changing the dynamics of culture. Even the idea of *success* is being redefined.

Success today is not simply having a nicer car or house than your neighbor. Rather, it's about impacting the way others see the world and react to it. It's about legacy! In fact, the most successful people I know are not laboring simply to increase their net worth. They definitely don't need another car or house, and they are not concerned about being able to afford their lifestyle. Rather, they want to build something that will remain. They want to complete a work they can be proud of when they leave this world.

It is generally accepted that seven cultural spheres dictate the norms of society—government, family, education, religion, business, entertainment, and media. These are the cultural mountains that many of us want to climb. God has placed a truth in us that has the capacity to make us like a city on a hill in one of these spheres (see Matt. 5:14). Before that can happen, much exploratory work needs to be done so that we can clarify our message and the lies our truths are meant to dispel. It's worth it, though! The advancement of the Kingdom in our generation and those to come hinges on our ability to displace the idols (lies) the devil has planted on these mountains.

Our job is to turn the places where these idols are worshiped into demonstrations of God's glory, just as Elijah did. I'm not suggesting we call fire from Heaven on the local TV network. However, the media does propagate certain lies, and these lies need to be replaced with God's truth. The same is true of each of these mountains. We must gain our salt back. We must shine our light. Christ in us—the hope of glory to be revealed (see Col. 1:27)—is challenging the Church today with a conquering spirit. He is searching for those who will follow the compulsion to seek and find their places on these mountains. God has been working toward a restoration of the environment of the Garden of Eden—where humanity walked with Him—ever since the failure of Adam.

Christ came from Heaven, lived on earth, and endured the cross. Then, He fought through hell and the grave to ensure His legacy and fulfill the will of our heavenly Father. Jesus left behind a seed that was first planted in the Church and is still thriving and growing today. We are that seed. We are the legacy of Jesus. He has chosen us to enforce His will and dominion on earth as it is in Heaven. We are the ones called to demonstrate to the world that He was sent from the Father of all creation.

Despite this, many Christians have inaccurate beliefs about

money. Generally, money and Christians have not been friends. Many churches and ministries seem to have a cultural subconscious that says money is not good if it's not in the offering plate. Many pastors and teachers only speak of giving or sowing. I have a few questions about this. First, why don't we hear more teaching about reaping? Second, why aren't churches run with a goal of self-sufficiency? Why isn't profitability a fundamental guideline for a church or Christian organization? Third, wouldn't we be much more effective if we applied some economic principles to our decision-making processes as individuals and organizations? Wouldn't we accomplish much more and have an opportunity to see the true fulfillment of Jesus' words in the great commission if we understood a bit about business, investing, and ourselves?

My goal is to answer all of these questions and to address much of the nagging uncertainty that many in the Church have been faced with. In Luke 16, Jesus shares a parable about a man who was losing his job. This man was later commended by his boss for being wise. Afterward, Jesus says, "The sons of this world are more shrewd in dealing with their own generation than the sons of light" (Luke 16:8). I read this in my late teens, while praying one day, and God spoke to me. He said, "Notice I didn't say it had to be this way. I was simply making an observation." I prayed and committed that day, "If You will help me, I will make sure I am not one of those people."

Many of us procrastinate in *uncertainty*, not because we are afraid, even though we may be fearful. We have not jumped into our calling because we have many questions and decisions that must be addressed. Regretfully, we have been unable to identify all of the resources needed to connect those dots. In Luke 6:46–49, Jesus prefaces a parable with these words: "Whoever comes to Me, and hears My sayings and does them, I will show you whom he is like" (NKJV). Then, He says that following His teachings is like digging a deep foundation for a house that will remain against any trial and withstand every storm. This is my goal here—to give you a pick axe and shovel so that you can not only explore the law that's written in your heart but also move forward with wisdom as you climb that mountain.

The wisdom I offer you is, of course, the fruit of my own journey to climb the mountain. For me, it began when I was just eight years old, and tragedy struck, turning my family upside down. One evening, we attended the mid-week service at our church, which was a small Baptist church that my grandfather had started decades earlier. Afterward, my brother, Ricky, complained that his stomach was hurting. The next day, I stayed home from school with Ricky and my mom to care for him. We were so close that my parents would let me stay home from school because of the immense concern I had if Ricky was sick.

Around 10 a.m., my mom and I began discussing Ricky and wondering why he wasn't up yet. When we went to the bedroom to check on him, we found him lying on his back with a purple hue to his skin. He was barely conscious but had a peaceful look to his face. After much effort and help from a neighbor we got him into the car and raced to the hospital. While my mom drove to the hospital, I held Ricky in my arms to keep him from choking. I kept talking to him, trying to keep him conscious. He fell limp in my arms on the way to the hospital. When we arrived, the medical staff worked to save him for hours and hours. He was on life support for several days, and my parents didn't sleep that entire time.

On the night we took Ricky to the hospital, before I went to sleep at the house of a family friend, I prayed and asked God to heal Ricky. It was the most genuine prayer an eight-year-old could pray. Ricky was my brother, my hero, and my best friend. God wrapped His arms around me that night. I felt an overwhelming love and peace, and I knew everything was going to be OK. Yet, a few days later I attended Ricky's funeral, completely devastated. My family was in shock for quite some time afterward. Ever since that night, I have been held in the arms of my heavenly Father. This experience of His arms and His overwhelming love and peace birthed in me an intense desire to not only please Him but to show Him to others. Now, more than thirty years later, I still long to show His beauty to the world. For me, the way this works out is in the business realm.

Earlier, I noted Jesus' observation in Luke 16 that secular men and women in business are often wiser than those who represent Him. This was something I could not accept. I felt compelled to show the world that God and His followers are greater. Because of this, I devoted myself to studying business, economics, finance, investing, and various peripheral subjects related to success in business. It seems like I have been Moses investigating burning bushes on many different occasions. I would find myself curious about a book I saw the title of or a subject someone mentioned, and as I looked at it, the bush would speak to me. In other words, God spoke to me from that book or subject.

I've been in figurative pits and prisons. I've run from Saul, even though I had a chance to kill him, and I have wrestled at the ford of Jabok, only to find someone else looking at me in the mirror. My passion for God has led me on a journey, and I have found some treasures that I want to pass on to you. This book, even though it is short, is not just the tip of the iceberg on a lot of different subjects. Rather, I have gone to the depths of these icebergs and hulled out a chunk that has taken me over twenty years of research and prayer to find. Those are the pieces I'm going to share with you here. Some are the revelations that fashion my perspective when navigating the markets or financial decisions. Some are truths about the way markets, economics, business, and even our minds work.

If you apply these treasures to your thought processes, they will empower you to shine as a city on a hill. You will be able to endure any challenge thrown your way, to persevere with wisdom when conflicting information comes your way. Financial and business decisions will become much simpler and intuitive. You'll be like a baseball player who seems to effortlessly hit a home run. Your decisions will become instinctive as you are led by the Spirit.

The Holy Spirit guides us into all truth (see John 16:13). This promise comes with responsibility on our part. How can we be guided if we're sitting still? Here, I'm giving a guided tour of what God has shown me to be critical in the process of climbing our mountains. We have the burning desire to impact our generation for the Kingdom of Heaven. God had a dream when He was fashioning the world, and He placed the roles each of us is destined to play in that dream inside us. My goal is to provide some critical tools for that journey.

Whether you're in the field of finance, education, government, entertainment, media, religion, or family, where your treasure is, there your heart will be also (see Matt. 6:21). In other words, the status of your treasure is and will be a reflection of your heart. These tools I am about to share with you will not only apply to your investing and business planning decisions, but they will also shine light onto the field you are called to. They will be like a Swiss army knife that you can carry in your pocket and use when working with clients, voters, investors, patients, students, and even your own family. Let's begin our journey.

DECLARATION

I am committed to climbing my mountain with determination and courage, knowing that I can do all things through Christ who strengthens me (see Phil 4:13).

MOUNTAIN CLIMBING STEPS

1. Which of the seven mountains (spheres) are you most passionate about or interested in?

2. What aspect of that mountain are you most concerned with?

3. What steps have you taken in your life so far to influence that mountain?

CHAPTER 1

WHAT'S THE POINT?

In Luke 12:16–21, we read the story of a man who was living a life of abundance. Because of his abundance, he thought to himself, *What should I do with this excess?* His solution was to build more storage barns in order to protect his wealth. Not only did he build larger barns, but he also demolished the ones in existence. Through building larger storage areas and increasing his wealth, he came to the conclusion that he could find rest and relaxation. He could retire. Retirement has become the dream of civilization, but it appears that God has a different idea in mind. In fact, in the context of this story, Jesus says, "One's life does not consist in the abundance of his possessions" (Luke 12:15). In this parable, God was so displeased with this man's attitude and actions that he called him "Fool!" and required his life.

Jesus concludes this parable by saying, "So is the one who lays up treasure for himself and is not rich toward God" (Luke 12:21). Here is a picture of the war over our hearts: God vs. mammon; faith vs. flesh; Kingdom vs. selfishness. The battle rages. While this story is often used to criticize the wealthy, it should rather be used as a mirror to examine each of our souls.

The other side of this discussion is the belief that pious poverty leads to greater holiness. This was a popular theme during the early 1900s and is still pervasive today in some circles. Giving all to the poor and living in humble means is still viewed as especially holy by some. Jesus did tell the rich young ruler to do this (see Matt. 19:16–22); however, He did so based on the condition of that young man's heart. This was not a universal statement for all people. Otherwise, Jesus would not have stressed the importance of stewardship and production in other places. For example, Jesus condemned a fig tree for not being productive (see Matt. 21:19). And the man who didn't produce with the talent he was given was stripped of it (see Matt. 25:14–30). I don't think he would have escaped judgment if he had given it to the poor, either.

The idealization of poverty breaks down quickly with a simple question: Will we see a transformation in society if we take the wealth of Christian business owners and distribute it as a religious welfare program among the poor? I think not. We need a fresh perspective regarding wealth and wealth creation. Some people have been given a grace to create wealth, but what is missing, at times, is a purpose greater than attaining bigger net worth or accounts.

So many people are working and saving for future college expenses, a second home, or the sacred retirement. They dream of golf, travel, and a life of leisure. For many, this is the American dream. I am not suggesting that enjoying the fruit of your labor is bad or that financial planning is evil (after all, that's my day job). Nor am I saying that financial independence is evil or that we should not make it our goal. Financial wisdom is actually throughout the Bible. For example, in Romans, Paul says that we should "owe no one anything except to love each other..." (Rom. 13:8). In the Old Testament, the children of Israel were so enthralled by the restoration of the walls of Jerusalem (representing the Kingdom) that they declared they would "forego the crops of the seventh year and the exaction of every debt" (Neh. 10:31). That is real wealth—to be able to *not* reap a harvest every seven years *and* forgive the debts that were owed to them every seven years. They were living in abundance!

The difference we need is perspective. The rich man in Luke 12 was condemned due to his lack of Kingdom purpose. The wealth didn't drive him to that place either. It appears that he was like this all his life. Jesus said that a branch that does not produce fruit will be cast into the fire. I'm convinced God wants to create a machine, a system of wealth creation and the purpose-driven activation of it. Distributing to the poor and helpless is great, but we also need to impact the culture, which in turn will provide an environment of opportunity and hope to the needy. Christian Kingdom principles impact the lives of all who are in their vicinity. The fact that we are disciples of Christ places a greater demand on us that goes beyond our own capabilities. It takes us to a place where we are accountable to God's will, not just our credit score. Are we working to increase the size of our estate or to leave treasures in Heaven? I'm convinced that God has devised a strategy where wealth will be used as a tool to fund His will in this time. We must move beyond offerings on Sunday and into cultural vision with wealth.

Jesus said that all of the law and the prophets could be summed up in loving God and our neighbors (see Matt. 22:37-40). The condition of our hearts must be driven by love, but that's just where the Kingdom begins. It does not end with love; it ends with dominion, with all of God's enemies being made His footstool and all of the lies propagated in society being dispelled by the blinding light of His Kingdom. Healing, miracles, signs, and wonders are simply testimonies from Heaven; they are not the goal. Subdue and have dominion was the first goal, which was given by God to Adam, and it remains today as a command of His will and a promise for those who partake in it. Jesus' command to take up our cross and follow

Him still applies today, but not just in morality, as some would say (see Matt. 16:24).

Political campaigns require money. Educational reform requires money. Transformation in the messages our kids receive from TV, movies, and radio requires money. The list goes on and on. If we want to impact the things we complain about in our society, we need money. Certainly, some people will find themselves positioned to influence kings, like Daniel and Joseph. But others will become kings and have the wisdom to strategically align the resources that come with their position with the purpose of Heaven. Money is not evil; it's a tool. Historically, social and cultural changes have taken decades to evolve. Because of this, we must think strategically and move forward with wisdom, focus, and the necessary resources. We must not accept things as they are and look for a way to escape. Nor should we sit around waiting for someone else to lead the charge. God is waiting for us!

God is raising up a tribe of people like Joshua and Caleb who are not afraid of the grasshoppers that others call "giants." God is beginning to outline strategies that will empower us and set us free to subdue and have dominion on earth as it is in Heaven. Christ's authority in Heaven is ours to enforce on earth, and we are preparing for the most victorious time the Church has seen in history. It's time to take our mountains, to embrace our vision, to take up our cross. God is outlining actionable steps that will propel us onto the mountain tops of our generation.

This book is about the financial aspects and principles that are required to climb that mountain. We don't need to know all of the answers, but we do need to have the right disciplines and know how to speak the right language. Stewardship, insight, knowledge, and the Spirit of God are critical to our success. May God give us a deep, burning passion for His Kingdom and His righteousness! Let us begin with a deep sense that the Father of all existence has a will for our time, lives, and resources. Let us look to Him to order our steps and dedicate ourselves to lives of stewardship worthy of increase.

DECLARATION

As for me, my house, and my resources, we will serve the Lord
(see Josh. 24:15).

MOUNTAIN CLIMBING STEPS

4. What, if any, focus have you had with your resources that does not align with your mountain mission?

5. How committed are you to moving forward with that mission?

6. What obstacles interfere with your ability to move forward?

CHAPTER 2

ATTACK A GOD-SIZED ENEMY

I've heard many sermons and personal development presentations that talk as if becoming wealthy is easy and should be normal. A lot of Christian preachers speak as if all you have to do is have faith and, of course, God will make you rich. BOOM! There it is! I perceive this as a negative abuse of the faith movement. Some, in my opinion, took the revelations from that movement to an unhealthy extreme. God's not an ATM, and I don't know about you, but I don't spend much time with people who always have their hand out. I enjoy being around people who enjoy being around me. I love being generous and believe in helping a friend in need. True relationship goes much deeper than asking for hand-outs. This is true in our relationships with others and with God.

Our heavenly Father is not interested in having a co-dependent relationship with His kids. As a father, I want to raise children who exhibit independence as adults and excel in the craft of their choosing. I want to raise adults who can stand on their own and face tough challenges without running back to me to rescue them. I don't know any parents who have been faced with kids who returned home as mature adults who were proud of that. Sure, as parents we are here to support our kids, to a degree, when they get in trouble. But it is not what any parent wants. Not only do I want to raise mature adults, but I want to be in a position to open doors of opportunity for my children when they are adults. I want to provide connections and guidance, when possible, that will cause them to prosper as they mature. I'm not interested in paying their bills forever. That would just cripple them and hinder their ability to achieve their own destiny. I want to show them how their wings work and then let them fly.

This, I believe, is also God's goal for us as His kids. We see this in Deuteronomy 8:18, where God says to the Israelites:

> And you shall remember the LORD your God, for it is He who gives you power to get wealth, that He may establish His covenant which He swore to your fathers, as it is this day (NKJV).

Many people interpret this to mean that God gives us the ability to get wealth and we should, therefore, expect it. The problem is that in the context of this Scripture God was rebuking Israel for their arrogance. This was not an open-ended promise that relieved Israel—or us—of individual responsibility.

The general theme in the Bible is that God wants to bless the faithful—those who are called and who live according to His plan. His plan is one of the critical pieces that is missed, often because it's greater than we can ask or think. As Paul says, God "is able to do exceedingly abundantly above all that we ask or think, according to the power that works in us" (Eph. 3:20 NKJV). The Greek word translated here as *works* is *energeo,* which means "to effect" or "to put into operation" in us. It's a word of activation. God is activating us with His power.

As Third John 2 says, "Beloved, I pray that you may prosper in all things and be in health, just as your soul prospers." It all starts with us and the activation of God's calling, which is demonstrated when we achieve something we could not achieve on our own merit. The giants in the land aren't that big from Heaven's perspective. If we allow the nature of Christ in us to develop and activate, we can conquer nations and disciple a generation. God pointed out Jericho and said to Joshua, "I have given you this land." Once we take charge of the land of our hearts, then God can give us the land of grasshopper-sized giants.

See, according to the context in Deuteronomy 9, God wants us to attack a *big* enemy—one that we cannot overcome, but that He can, if we act accordingly. That was the key to Israel's success and wealth. And it's the key to the next financial level for each one of us. What are our goals?

- To get a good job and pay the bills, with maybe a little savings along the way?
- To have successful businesses and hopefully give a good testimony?
- To be able to be generous?

All of these are good things, but God has an agenda today, and He's looking for people to place as a city on a hill (or mountain). I am convinced that those who feel called to the business mountain, especially, will find in their hearts a desire for something more. (I'll deal with that in the final section of this book.)

In Sunday school, at a very young age, I learned about David overcoming Goliath. I imagined, as portrayed by the teacher, that David slung that stone and God miraculously caused it to strike Goliath fatally. But that's not what happened. David had skills. He was a marksman with his sling. In ancient times, many armies included a troop of slingers who served as short-range artillery. David, of course, was a young man, but he was talented none the less. I believe he had developed a marksman skill level with his sling shot. Then, he found himself within earshot of the giant's threats, which caused everyone else to fear. The giant was challenging anyone to an up-close and personal brawl to the death. No one wanted anything to do with that, and they were frozen by the fear of their own demise. David, being the faith-filled young man that he was, refused to give in to that fear. He could not tolerate the boastfulness of this Philistine. He had to do something, so he fought with his familiar weapon, knowing that God was with him and would stand at his side.

Just as He did with David, God has given you some natural abilities. Other abilities you have developed through your life. He has also given you a burning desire to deal with a loud mouth shouting from a valley. Look at what frustrates and makes you angry about your industry or society. You have some gear in your bag that can take that enemy down with the strength of God's hand, and I'm going to give you a few more weapons here.

Financial literacy and discipline are key tools in achieving earth-flipping, generation-changing impact. We must learn the ways of Babylon to succeed there. That's what this book is about. "Follow the money" is a common saying in business and politics. People are often driven by a desire for greed or power. If we know the rules of the game and have supernatural insight from the Holy Spirit, we will have a chance at winning and find ourselves as a city on a hill. If we don't know the rules, we are doomed to flounder in obscurity and never move into the greatness we were created for. We are going to change that!

Earlier we mentioned Jesus' statement in Luke 16 about the business prowess of the people of the world. Let's look at the context:

> For the sons of this world are more shrewd in their generation than the sons of light....He who is faithful in what is least is faithful also in much; and he who is unjust in what is least is unjust also in much. Therefore if you have not been faithful in the unrighteous mammon, who will commit to your trust the true riches? (Luke 16:8; 10–11 NKJV).

We are required to understand and exercise faithfulness in small things before we can be trusted with mountain tops. This is crucial. Jesus' words here are like a blueprint for success in our lives. This is how we lay a foundation that we can stand on, so that when we conquer our giants and take our promised land, we will be prepared. We will not be blown away by the challenges and decisions we will face. We must be wise as serpents in business and financial matters. And we must be filled with a heart of love for our heavenly Father and this generation. We must be filled with passion for our place in His master plan. God needs you to be able to hit a home run when it's your turn at the plate; I'm going to teach you how to swing.

God has a greater place for you. But first, He wants a strong foundation built on stewardship and a heart that's willing for risk to be your calling card. Ask yourself, *Am I attacking a God-sized enemy?* If you are ready, step up with a stone in your hand and expect amazing things!

DECLARATION

I can conquer any enemy, for God is with me and no one can stand against me (see Rom 8:31).

MOUNTAIN CLIMBING STEPS

7. Does the issue or lie you want to attack seem a bit overwhelming? (It should.)

8. What grasshopper-sized obstacles stand in your way?

9. What activity can you do today that will begin your progress up the mountain?

CHAPTER 3

SERVANT, SON, ONE

We all must serve to be great in the Kingdom. Jesus said a heart of service toward all is a prerequisite to significance in the Kingdom of Heaven. Matthew 20:16, where Jesus says, "The last will be first, and the first last," is often used to inspire people to serve in the local church. Certainly, serving in the church is important. I have seen an enormous amount of growth in my life from serving in local churches. I served a prophet and received an amazing impartation as a result. However, here I want to take a different angle on this verse and deal with our perspective of our heavenly Father and our community within the body of Christ.

We often see ourselves as servants to our brothers and sisters in Christ. That's absolutely scriptural. I believe strongly in serving and generosity in the body of Christ. However, God has not intended us to be servants alone. I believe He intends a progression to take place, so that we do not view ourselves simply in light of our obedience as servants. Perspective is a powerful thing. We see this in Jesus' warning to His disciples in Luke 8:18: "Therefore take heed how you hear. For whoever has, to him more will be given; and whoever does not have, even what he seems to have will be taken from him" (NKJV). In this verse, the word *hear* comes from a Greek word that means "to take in, admit to, mental acceptance; to hear, heed, obey." In other words, it is our perception of a message and the acceptance of it in our minds that it is real or true. Therefore, we must be careful *how* we perceive and *what* we accept as truth. If we only see ourselves as servants, then we will be limited to the actions and impact a servant can have.

I bought a house a few months ago and hired a contractor to paint the interior and patch some holes. I also paid a carpet installer to deliver and install carpet that I had purchased. These companies were providing a service that was extremely important to me. I wanted these projects completed prior to moving in, so timely completion was critical. But, no matter how important these projects were to me, these contractors are not included in my estate. If they were in trouble and needed support in some fashion, my response to a request would be limited, but they probably would not be calling me unless they had a question regarding a financial matter. Any extreme requests would not be appropriate because of the nature of our relationship.

In recent times, some in the Church have begun to have an elevated view of our relationship with our "Papa God," as they say. God is our Father, as much as Christ is His Son. Jesus came as a man to restore people to the place of God's original intent. We have begun to see our Holy Father as a dear, loving, embracing Father who cares for His children more than the lilies of the field. God is the Father to the fatherless. He is our Father, whether we have loving parents or not. It's wonderful to think of our God in these terms. It is a truth that should be completely embraced. God is always loving toward us. The only question is whether we can perceive it or not. I'm convinced there is a higher place in Heaven's perspective, though.

The nature of our relationship with our Heavenly Father must be expanded. As John 17:20–23 says:

> I do not pray for these alone, but also for those who will believe in Me through their word; that they all may be one, as You, Father, are in Me, and I in You; that they also may be one in Us, that the world may believe that You sent Me. And the glory which You gave Me I have given them, that they may be one just as We are one: I in them, and You in Me; that they may be made perfect in one, and that the world may know that You have sent Me, and have loved them as You have loved Me (NKJV).

Here Jesus prays for us, something I believe He continues to do today. In His prayer, He gives us this formula: We become *one* with each other, and in Christ *one* with God, our Father. The goal of this oneness is "that the world may know that You have sent Me."

Being one with Heaven is not only an experience of God's presence during worship or prayer. Rather, it is a perception that leads to certain behavior which produces results. All of creation is groaning for the "revealing of the sons of God" (Rom. 8:19). I'm convinced this is bigger than praying for a few people in our lifetime. Jesus healed the sick and raised the dead to send a message. It was a testimony about who He was, but He did not come to heal multitudes alone. He was on a much larger mission—to reconcile people to Heaven. Miracles were a sign of who He was and who He was One with. Miracles were not the goal, but the testimony to the goal. His mission was always to "be about My Father's business" (Luke 2:49 NKJV).

Our mission as Christians is not to have a testimony on Sunday morning about how many people we have prayed for or to brag about our success in business or other fields. Rather, our mission is to be about our Father's business, His original intent for humankind, which is to subdue and have dominion. God had all authority in Heaven and on earth long before they existed. Christ came to restore that authority to us so that His Kingdom will be enforced on earth, as was the original intent with Adam. We must, however, unify behind the mission of Heaven to see the fullness of this on display.

I could say much more about this. What is important, if we are ever to reach unity, is that we realize that we must move beyond restrictive theologies and embrace one another in love. Jesus went so far as to say, "By this all will know that you are My disciples, if you have love for one another" (John 13:35 NKJV). This is our calling card, but love is often misunderstood. I love my kids, but if I sit around and tell them that all the time, I will create codependent relationships that are crippling to them. I must model, teach, and encourage growth, responsibility, vision, diligence, and other aggressive and action-oriented characteristics. What if we took that perspective with each other? What if we truly held each other in higher esteem than we do ourselves? What if we were to unite behind a mission that exceeds our next paycheck or business venture?

If one can cast out a thousand and two can cast out ten thousand (see Deut. 32:30), imagine what could happen if believers united behind a mission to "subdue and have dominion." It took eleven disciples to initiate a movement that turned the world of the first century upside down (see Acts 17:6). Our modern world could use some reconfiguring, too. That's what being one with God is about. When we are united with Him and one another, we begin to see ourselves as part of the grand plan of Heaven. God has chosen a people in this generation to reshape society. As we unite behind this mission, we will see the timing, wisdom, and resources of our heavenly Father supply all that we need to accomplish His good works. God desires friends who share His perspective on earth, not indentured servants. He wants us to stand up for His intentions and take the gates of Hell by force.

I had a vision many years ago in which I was taken into a room beyond a veil. A large angel stood guard at the veil, prior to where one entered the room. He pulled back the veil, and though he didn't utter a word, I knew I was being invited in. When I entered, I saw the ark of the covenant with menorah lighting the room from the corners and a man with the body of a lamb standing behind it. The wool coat of the lamb was dirty, matted, and bloodied as he stood on two feet. He looked as if he had been beaten badly and cut. However, there was no indication of weakness, as he walked to the right side of the ark (my left). I began to lose control of my emotions and weep, while falling to my knees as I felt the presence of God overwhelming me. A voice spoke to me and said, "Look at his face." I had to focus, because it was shrouded in shadow. As I gained sight of his face, I was alarmed to see it was me. God spoke to me at that moment of confusion and said, "You must see yourself the way I see you, so the world can see."

Clearly, there is only one Messiah—Jesus—who was the original sacrifice and the firstborn of many brethren (see Rom. 8:29). However, *we* are His anointed ones. We are the ones who are chosen to fulfill, in our generation, the work He began long ago. We must take on the same diligence and veracity of commitment that Jesus demonstrated in allowing the Father to fulfill every good work in Him and His actions. We need that commitment to be identified and to dominate in every field in our lives.

This reminds me of the poem, "Footprints in the Sand." In it, a man faces challenging circumstances. Later, he learns from Jesus that during his struggles, when he could not identify two sets of footprints, he was being carried by Christ. This poem presents an image of our relationship with our heavenly Father and His son Jesus Christ that has caused Christians to be focused on a rescue from above. We expect God to deliver us from evil times and struggles when they occur. Although at times I have seen God's hand deliver me from challenging circumstances, I believe there is a higher place and perspective that God wants us to attain.

Imagine that same walk on the beach with Christ. However, the direction we are headed is directly aligned with the calling from Heaven on our lives. We are moving forward in the field we have been chosen for. We are seeking first the Kingdom, as Christ directed, and we are pursuing the purpose God has placed inside our hearts. As we walk down that path, we come to a point of decision. We have a building to purchase, a candidacy to attain, a business to pursue, or any other venture we have been dreaming about. As we acknowledge that the intention to pursue that goal was Heaven-sent, we will find that the provision we need for that occasion will be present as we pursue it. We must take action, however, both spiritual (prayer, worship, declarations, fasting, etc.) and physical (planning, saving, investing, etc.). As we walk on this journey, we will begin to see earth and the substance of it align with God's intentions. Our oneness with God is reflected in the fulfillment of His will on earth through our actions.

Our finances are a big part of that. Jesus says, "For where your treasure is, there your heart will be also" (Matt. 6:21 NKJV). I believe the condition and focus of our finances will demonstrate where our hearts are directed. Let's align our hearts and resources with the mission from Heaven. Out of that, our identity in Christ will be expanded as we join arms together.

DECLARATION

I am one with God in Christ and, therefore, anything I need for my mountain mission is at my disposal
(see 2 Pet. 1:3).

MOUNTAIN CLIMBING STEPS

10. What areas of your life seem less than ideal?

11. In what areas of your life are you waiting for God to do some thing, but taking no action of your own?

12. What are you afraid of?

CHAPTER 4

THINK LIKE A STEWARD

It's always good to know what you're getting into. Christ gave us an amazing example of this. He understood what He was faced with from the beginning of time, yet He *chose* to fulfill it to the pleasure of the Father. We are all the beneficiaries of the grace that Christ fulfilled by committing Himself to the Father's will.

Along these lines, Luke 14:28–32 contains two parables about preparedness. The first is about building a tower. Jesus says it only makes sense to calculate the cost of building the tower prior to beginning the building process. For example, one must get several quotes on the project, understand building codes and zoning, and locate the appropriate skilled labor and materials. All of these provide the opportunity to evaluate one's ability to complete the project. If a person fails to do this, as Jesus puts it, "When he has laid a foundation and is not able to finish, all who see it begin to mock him, saying, 'This man began to build and was not able to finish'" (Luke 14:29–30).

The second parable is about a king who is about to enter a battle. He would be wise to first evaluate the military strength of his opponent. Otherwise, he risks a potentially devastating defeat that could result in the loss of his military might and possibly his kingdom. It would be better for that king to offer a truce and attempt terms of peace in advance if he is not able to overtake his adversary.

These parables give fantastic examples of the importance of evaluation and planning. In context, they tell us that following Christ and His teachings requires this evaluation. Just before this, Jesus says, "Whoever does not bear his own cross and come after me cannot be my disciple" (Luke 14:27). And at the end of these parables, He sums up His point by saying, "So[!] therefore, any one of you who does not renounce all that he has cannot be my disciple"(Luke 14:33). Put it all together, and it seems that following Christ and chasing after our place in the Kingdom is something to be considered before we commit.

Jesus then goes on to say, "Salt is good, but if salt has lost its taste, how shall its saltiness be restored? It is of no use... It is thrown away. He who has ears to hear, let him hear" (Luke 14:34–35). Of course, I am not referring to our faith in Christ as the Son of God or the salvation we receive from Him as something we should evaluate prior to accepting. Clearly, by faith we are saved. There is nothing to evaluate there. Rather, what we need to evaluate is our commitment to discipleship and activation in the Kingdom. These we may attain after we receive salvation by faith. On this journey, let us fully consider what is required of us and then soberly commit to fulfill it.

Likewise, to evaluate financial decisions that affect our calling, we must have clarity, not doubt. As James says, a double-minded man is unstable in all his ways (see James 1:8). Any doubt in our capacity or any lack of willingness will cripple us. Instead, we need to hear Jesus calling us and jump out of our boat of safety, as Peter did when Jesus called to him on the raging sea. His call gives us confidence to move forward in faith. Then, we can commit to following through to see His purposes accomplished on earth. Our willingness to take personal responsibility is a big part of this.

Personal responsibility is talked about throughout the Bible, and in a particular way, it is emphasized in the teachings of Christ. The parable of the talents reiterates the importance of being productive. At one point, Jesus says that unfruitfulness will be condemned to the fire (see Luke 13:6–9). This should provoke sober thoughtfulness, holy reverence, and at the same time, immense gratitude that we have the opportunity to not just take part in His blessings but be raised up with Him in the calling of His labor and mission for humankind. Counting the cost is about taking one step at a time, with a constant evaluation of focus, and continuing to sharpen that focus on Him and what brings Him joy in the earth. This is where stewardship begins. It is a humbling, yet also a strengthening of the spirit. It involves the resolve to follow. It says, "If He chose me, then I will be a willing vessel." When we commit to fully expressing all that He has given us, we can be confident that we will have the resources necessary to fulfill the calling.

STEWARDSHIP 101

Doing something for the benefit of others is admirable. Performing a service in the name of God or for the betterment of humanity is noble, and such acts are often immortalized in history books. I love reading about the founding fathers of our great nation. John Adams is my favorite. He suffered immensely in the service of our fledgling republic, including being separated from his family for years at a time while his wife and children suffered. He was neglected and unappreciated by the citizens and cause he strove to serve. However, even in discouragement, he continued to serve. His wife, Abigail, was a tremendous picture of stewardship. She tended to the kids in sickness and hard winters. Continuing to support her husband in his cause, she increased the wealth of her family while he was away serving his country. They both demonstrated a great deal of resolve to see the dream of America come true.

History books are full of stories of those who overcame tremendous odds to accomplish their goals. Those who sacrificed for God and country continue to be discussed hundreds of years later, in schools around the world today. Stewardship begins with the acknowledgement that there is something more important than us—something bigger than ambition, pride, selfishness, and greed. Of course, stewardship is not about sacrifice alone. Rather, it's about surrendering to a vision. It says that all else can fall away, but this one thing will remain. God has given us the beautiful opportunity to follow in Christ's example of surrender. However, surrender isn't defined by poverty and lowliness. Often, these are cloaks of arrogance and pride. Being broke is not a reflection of commitment to Christ. Rather, it is often a result of being committed to selfishness. If we sow to the flesh, we will reap death, which includes the death of our bank accounts (see Gal. 6:8). But, since the sparrows have no worry for their next meal, we should not either (see Matt. 10:29–31). In other words, those who practice following Christ in stewardship will eat well!

Stewardship begins in the heart. It begins with accepting that everything we are and have was given to us to be a resource for worship. In Exodus 10:24–26, Pharaoh becomes frustrated by the plagues that are inflicting the Egyptians because he refuses to let the Israelites go. Eventually, he tells Moses, "Go, serve the LORD; your little ones also may go with you; only let your flocks and your herds remain behind" (Exod. 10:24). But Moses responds:

> You must also let us have sacrifices and burnt offerings, that we may sacrifice to the LORD our God. Our livestock also must go with us; not a hoof shall be left behind, for we must take of them to serve the LORD

> our God, and we do not know with what we must serve the LORD until we arrive there (Exodus 10:25–26).

Two very different perspectives are represented here. Pharaoh wanted to control the wealth, no doubt because he thought that by controlling their assets he would control the Hebrew people and continue his reign over them. Moses presents a much different picture. He knew that their resources were tools that would be used to worship the Lord. He couldn't even be sure what God would require as a sacrifice, and therefore, was not willing to leave a single hoof, just in case God would find pleasure in it. As it did with Moses, being relentlessly dedicated will often place us in someone's crosshairs. Others may not understand, particularly if they are under the sway of demonic forces as Pharaoh was. Nevertheless, we must dedicate ourselves to maintaining the perspective that it's all His—whether or not our friends, family, and enemies can see where we are headed. Eventually, if we maintain our focus, we will find ourselves standing on a mountain top worshiping in spirit and in truth. Stewardship is ultimately about worship.

God's will and purpose in our lives and our generation must have the highest value in our hearts. That's the heart of stewardship in the Kingdom. It is serious business. We must not say, "It's all His" and then go about our days as usual. Unfortunately, this phrase has often been used as a cliché, with no manifestation of results. Instead, stewardship involves adorning ourselves with the yoke that's put before us and taking up our cross—our part, including our money, time, attention, energy, and talents. We must surrender them all to what is important to Him, resolutely carrying out the pleasure of the King and His desires for our lives. That is true stewardship.

The question, just like in Luke 14, isn't whether we should commit to something unrealistic. That answer is unequivocally *no.* Instead, the question is whether we will commit wholeheartedly to

God's mission. The Bible tells us we cannot serve two masters. We will serve the one and hate the other (see Matt. 6:24). We cannot be committed to both God's will and to our own selfish desires. Only one can be our master. Because of this, we need to re-center our lives on His heart and purpose. The answer will always be to use our tools, resources, talents, and ultimately our hearts to fulfill the things that brings Him joy.

This, of course, does not mean we should just serve indiscriminately. We can be completely out of alignment with God's will while serving good causes. The key is to serve in the right places and to use our talents for the right purposes. Thus, saying *no* is part of stewardship. Billionaire Warren Buffet was once asked what separates the successful from the ultra-successful. He said that those who achieve the highest tiers in society say *no* more often. That is Kingdom stewardship! When we are focused, we will have a limited field of vision. We will not be available to help everyone. Even Jesus had to be convinced to serve at times. The centurion had to state his case and demonstrate his faith (see Matt. 8:5–13). The Canaanite woman had to overcome offense and refuse to relent (see Matt. 15:21–28). It is crucial that we say *no* to the things that will distract us. The path is straight and narrow, and only a few will follow it (see Matt. 7:13–14).

We may admire those who commit their lives to foreign ministry in third world countries. However, it's not the context that drives stewardship; it's the task laid before us by the King. If I'm called to change the context of finances in the Body of Christ, but I sell everything I have, give it to the poor, and dedicate myself to traditional foreign ministry work, I have failed the heart of God. This is why we *must* be clear about the calling on our lives and not allow the frames presented by others to diminish that calling. The master of the universe is waiting for us to stand up in the place He has designated for us so that the world can see the beauty of Christ and His chosen ones.

MAKING BEAUTIFUL MUSIC

I am not a musician, and I cannot sing very well, but I *love* music. My instrument is the thousands of dollars worth of sound equipment that, as a sound man, I use at church. I don't know that I'm very good at it, but I do love it, and I've heard I'm OK. I do know that I care a great deal about the experience of both the musicians on stage and the audience. Mixing for worship is particularly special to me, because I feel I'm taking part in God receiving praise from hundreds of people at one time. I find a great deal of fulfillment and joy in getting the mix just right so that everyone can forget about everything except the music and the sweet aroma contained in it. How wonderful is that? I find my role very special, despite, hopefully, no one knowing I'm there. My commitments have limited my ability to participate as a sound engineer very often, but the sound booth will always have a special place in my heart.

Imagine the greatest musicians and singers in the world being on a stage together and playing every note in the most magnificent fashion. At the same time, millions are in attendance to hear this breathtaking creation. But there is one problem. The crowd can't hear, because the sound system is not being used properly! How disappointing and incomplete would that be? When it comes to sound, the right pieces must be placed exactly where they belong; otherwise, the puzzle doesn't fit. It becomes a mutation of beauty. The same is true of our callings. When we are placed in the function where we belong, something beautiful happens.

Paul talks about this in First Corinthians 12:1–13:13, emphasizing the importance of finding our place and fulfilling it with all of our heart. My left hand has never asked me, "Why don't you write with me this time?" It simply accepts its job. Every molecule was created to fulfill a purpose in earth. My desk, the energy flowing into the computer and lights, and even the air I am breathing right now all interact unknowingly with each other to create the opportunity for me to pursue the activity I'm involved in at the time. My computer will never object to what I'm writing; neither will my fingers. Each member of the equation is, without consideration, available to my commands.

People often describe us as clay in the hands of the Master Potter, based on Isaiah 64. The image of God sitting at the potter's wheel and fashioning His masterpiece has reinforced the idea that God continues to work on us, eventually forming us into His image. What we often miss is that a potter is creating a vessel—a tool to be filled up and used for distribution. Isaiah 64:8 says, "But now, O LORD, you are our Father; we are the clay, and you are our potter; we are all the work of your hand." We are shaped to be His vessels. And we are designed to accomplish His purposes, just as I can use a drinking glass in whatever way I see fit.

The key to "fitting in" in the Kingdom of Heaven and God's purpose is to identify our usefulness and be unrestrained in our willingness to fulfill that purpose. When God calls, we have an opportunity for stewardship. Often, we find ourselves staring at a need that we might be able to provide the answer to, but our fears and concerns can convince us that it was not His beckoning. Justifying inaction, we are led to fade away into unfruitfulness and lethargy. Let us rather submit ourselves willfully to His purposes.

Unlike my left index finger, I have the ability to choose whether to strike the "T" on my keyboard. That is the beauty of stewardship. I choose to either take the vessel I am at this time and make it available or to place myself on the shelf of life. I can either produce and multiply with the tools and talents I am now, or I can hide them in the earth, like the unfaithful steward in Matthew 25:14–30. When confronted by his master, the unfaithful steward said:

> Master, I knew you to be a hard man, reaping where you did not sow, and gathering where you scattered no seed, so I was afraid, and I went and hid your talent in the ground. Here you have what is yours (Matthew 25:24–25).

In the Bible, *earth* is commonly accepted as a metaphor for humanity or flesh. It is plain to me that the Master was upset with this servant for not making his talents available to the forces of multiplication that activity provides. Instead, he hid his talent. How many times have we been convinced that we are not ready or that someone else will do the task at hand? Why not offer? Why not be active? Why not place ourselves on the altar of what's in front of us?

Let us be guided by the greatest commandment in Matthew 22:37—"Love the Lord your God with all your heart and with all your soul and with all your mind." We overcome our earth by digging up those talents and bringing them into the sunlight as an offering of worship. As First Corinthians 13:13 tells us, "...the greatest of these is love." One could say that the "earth" we must release our talents from is any motivation that conflicts with love. Fear, insecurity, greed, jealousy, and so on—in one form or another—all suffocate our ability to contribute to the Kingdom and fulfill the role of "good and faithful servant" (Matt. 25:21).

Every day, I tell my eight-year-old son how proud I am of him when he wakes, throughout the day, and when he goes to bed. I shower him with kisses and hugs, showing how much I appreciate his growth and simply the fact that he is my "daddy's boy." This is an imperfect picture of our Father's attitude toward us. Our heavenly Father looks to praise us as good and faithful stewards every day. He is not looking to judge us for mistakes or for "overstepping" our place (as some of us have feared). Rather, He is looking for us to *do* so that He can bless us with His approval every day.

The necessary ingredient for the beautiful music we can all be part of is participation. Each instrument must be played, each vocal chord activated, so that every person can hear and enjoy. In First Corinthians 12:4–31, Paul shares about the importance of each member actively realizing the position they are currently given. We must all strive to surrender to the calling He has for us at this time. We are all one body. To cast off dysfunction, we must each be active in the role we are placed in at this time. Here is the key: We choose whether or not to be useful. God has not just given us choices in faith and sin. He has also given us the power to choose to be productive and to choose to present our talent to Him.

For a long time, I lived in fear. I was hiding my talent, just like many others. I was afraid of failing and being a disappointment to myself and others. Eventually, I realized that the musician does not sit down to strike the keys of the piano for the first time masterfully. In the same way, I should not expect that my service to Heaven will begin without imperfections. We must all grow into the purpose God has for us. And we must, in the meantime, be willing to do what our hands find to do. Much wisdom and freedom are found in the ability to laugh at ourselves when necessary, to enjoy the social scraped knees we endure. This will keep us from stopping and giving up. What is most important is that we keep moving.

DECLARATION

All of me and all that I possess are resources to reveal the Kingdom of Heaven and the glory of Christ!

MOUNTAIN CLIMBING STEPS

13. What are your three best skills? Think about what you can do better than most people.

14. What would others say are my three best attributes? Feel free to ask your closest friends.

15. How can you apply these skills and attributes toward the passion and mission that God has placed in your heart? What physical actions can you take? (Do not include prayer or worship; you're doing that already.)

— PART 2 —

FINANCIAL PLANNING

Financial planning is a topic I'm very passionate about. Over the course of my career, I've helped thousands of families and business owners build a degree of stability and freedom in their financial lives that they otherwise may not have known. I've helped successful small business owners who needed assistance in reducing their tax burdens, as well as single moms trying to protect their assets for their young children, and many others. Successful financial planning is the architectural drawing that creates the opportunity to sleep at night in your new home. It's the design by which the bridge is built so that new explorations can occur. If done well, it allows new visions for what's possible in our lifetime to develop. This develops into a stable foundation upon which we can move forward into our calling, at whatever stage we may be.

To move effectively, we need a general understanding of the basic premises of financial planning and the various areas it addresses. A real estate developer would never begin a building project without first having a very good estimate of the value of the project once it's completed and the total cost of building it, as well as ensuring he had secured the capital to fund it. That's just smart business. It's important to see our personal and business finances in the same light. It's not all about the return though, as we will discover in the following chapters.

DECLARATION

I make financial decisions on purpose!

MOUNTAIN CLIMBING STEPS

16. When have you made financial decisions without being certain it was in your best interest and in alignment with your mountain climbing mission?

17. Why did you make a financial decision without being fully convinced it was the best decision?

CHAPTER 5

INTRODUCTION TO FINANCIAL PLANNING

So many of us, including advisors, only focus on investment returns. Actually, depending on the survey, between 80 and 95 percent of all advisors claim to focus on investment management, which is focused on investment returns. This is absolutely important, but it is only a small piece of the overall recipe for success. You may be interested in beginning a new venture or focus for your life, which might require a dramatic restructuring of your assets. Or perhaps life has decided you're going to have a new venture, whether you like it or not. Financial planning is all about being prepared for what's next and successfully moving forward.

Different facets need to be adjusted based on what's important to you. As with creating a delightful Italian dish, it's all in the recipe. I'm not a chef by any stretch of the imagination. However, I do love a good meal. Not many new ingredients are being discovered these days. Instead, it is in the measurement and combination of the ingredients that creativity comes to life, making delightful dishes for all to enjoy. The right selection, measurement, and combination of ingredients can cause you to have a wonderful experience. The wrong mixture is disastrous.

To arrive at the right plan for each person's situation, financial planning addresses six primary areas:

- Cash Flow Management
- Contingency Planning
- Investment Planning
- Goal / Purpose Planning
- Tax Planning
- Legacy Planning

Financial planning also considers your ability to make good financial decisions. In fact, there is a school of psychology, known as behavioral finance, that pulls back the veil regarding the process our minds go through when making financial decisions. Without the right behaviors and the ability to maintain them, it's impossible to achieve a successful result in planning. The best investment portfolio will be blown up by over-spending. Your financial circumstances will never prosper (no matter how big your lottery winnings are) if you don't begin to develop the right behaviors. We'll explore this in more detail in part 3.

As well, there are basic wealth-building principles that, if you grasp them, will lead you to a prosperous journey up your mountain.

1. Be generous
2. Spend less than you make
3. Invest wisely
4. Get advice
5. Use debt sparingly

6. Plan, Plan, Plan
7. Invest in yourself and education

If you need additional support on this, mentors or a like-minded financial advisor can be wonderful assets. Having accountability that will push you to your best and highest is indispensable. Don't listen to people who just want to tell you that you're wrong, though. Don't allow yourself to fall for the trap of following the herd. Find a micro church and mentor that will provide insight, knowledge, and perspective and equip and challenge you to move forward on your mountain climb.

DECLARATION

I am responsible for the outcomes in my life, including the current and future status of my finances!

MOUNTAIN CLIMBING STEPS

18. Of the six areas of financial planning, what is your most underdeveloped area?

19. Of the seven wealth-building principles, what have you focused on the least?

20. Give a special offering in dedication to your journey toward building wealth. Treat this as a spiritual stake in the ground, so do it prayerfully and make it an amount that's significant to you.

CHAPTER 6

CASH FLOW MANAGEMENT

Cash flow is kind of like having an apple tree. Apples have seeds in them, and one can, over time, build an apple orchard by planning properly. Or, one can simply enjoy the apples as they come. Some will die, some will be eaten by animals, and others will not mature properly. Either way, one still has an apple tree, and that's something. However, one may not want to settle for that one tree. Such people ask, "How is that orchard built again?" It all starts with cash flow management. We will explore a few tools in the following pages that are extremely useful in this field. Having a budget is indispensable. The ability to understand a cash flow statement and balance sheet is also useful.

A budget is simple. You have X dollars of income each week, month, or year. Out of that, you have Y expenses that are required to live your life. This includes things like your charitable giving, savings, mortgage payment, insurance, food, gas in the car, and so forth. These are what we call non-discretionary expenses. These items can only be reduced so much, until it becomes unrealistic. Beyond a certain point, you become a different person. Typically people don't want to live in a one-bedroom apartment with a family of four unless they are forced to by their circumstances. I listed charitable giving as a non-discretionary expense, because as a Christian I believe giving and generosity are mandatory. I am not alone in this. Many of the richest and most successful people in the world have dedicated their fortunes to charity and say that giving was a fundamental key to their success.

Also, saving is a non-discretionary expense. You must save money, no matter how small a sum it may be. Otherwise, you can never progress or develop the right behaviors to see your dreams become reality. The discipline and vision demonstrated by this behavior cannot be stressed enough. This component is the one thing that, if in place, will prove you faithful in little so that you can become a ruler of much. Entertainment, toys, games, vacation, and the like are considered discretionary expenses. These can be stopped all together if needed, and if you have the right mindset, you'll still have a smile on your face.

I've developed a resource that will assist you in creating a budget (see the budget document at the end of this chapter). It's a great tool that will give you some direction with your seeds as they come off that apple tree. Enjoy some, spend wisely, and see your harvest produce abundance.

A cash flow statement is simple. It involves taking a look back at your actual spending over a period of time to see where your money went. You made a certain amount of income over the last three months, and you need be able to judge whether you were productive with your seeds. A budget is a goal or direction for where your money *will* be spent (future tense), where as a cash flow statement tells you where your money *was* spent (past tense).

If you don't judge yourself, you'll find out what it means that life judges you. Your climbing team will be a great resource in this. Be transparent with them, particularly your mentor. That will help you confront your true challenges and give you someone to celebrate your disciplined victories. A partner (non-spouse) will help you gain valuable wisdom for moving forward as well. You should have a non-spouse accountability partner, because you want someone who is not emotionally attached to your decisions. Plus, as a family you have developed certain ways of doing things. Your spouse is right in the thick of that and may be just as blind to the areas of struggle for your family as you are. Don't count your spouse out though. If your spouse is not on board with your decision, you will have rough days ahead, which can be avoided if you bring him or her along on the journey

A balance sheet is a scorecard of sorts. You line up your assets on one side and your liabilities on the other. You then subtract your liabilities (debts) from your assets, and the resulting number is your net worth. Keeping track of this will give you an opportunity to see if you're making progress and building your net worth or if you're successfully driving yourself off a cliff of debt.

The feedback you receive from these documents and your mountain-climbing mentor will be tremendous resources as you move forward toward your goals. I have included a series of tools that make it easy to build your own financial statements. Use them, update them, and share them, and you'll be on your way to building wealth and a strong financial future.

BUDGET EXAMPLE

AUGUST 2013		
	INCOME	August 2013 - INCOME
	Allocation	August 2013 - Allocation
	MONTHLY EXPENSES	August 2013 - MONTHLY EXPENSES
EXAMPLE		
	MONTHLY EXPENSES	Example - MONTHLY EX-PENSES
SEPTEMBER 2013		
	INCOME	September 2013 - Allocation
	Allocation	September 2013 - INCOME
	MONTHLY EXPENSES	September 2013 - MONTHLY EXPENSES
OCTOBER 2013		
	INCOME	October 2013 - INCOME
	Allocation	October 2013 - Allocation
	MONTHLY EXPENSES	October 2013 - MONTHLY EXPENSES

INCOME

DESCRIPTION	PROJECTED INCOME FOR THE MONTH	INCOME RECEIVED	DIFFERENCE
HUSBAND'S PAYCHECK	$4000.00	$4157.00	$157.00
WIFE'S PAYCHECK	$4000.00	$4240.00	$240.00
RENTAL	$750.00	$750.00	$0.00
TOTAL	$8750.00	$9147.00	$397.00

ALLOCATION

	HOW MUCH INCOME SPENT	ACTUAL EXPENSE ALLOCATION	ACTUAL PAID	DIFF	ACTUAL DISCRE-TIONARY
RATIO	62%				
HUSBAND		$0.00	$3283.16	$3283.16	$4000.00
WIFE		$0.00	$2800.00	$2800.00	$4750.00
TOTAL		$0.00	$6083.16	$6083.16	$8750.00

EXPENSES

DESCRIPTION	PROJECTED	ACTUAL
MORTGAGE	$2000.00	$2100.00
VERIZON	$250.00	$243.75
CAR LOAN	$533.00	$533.00
CAR LEASE	$451.00	$451.00
UTILITIES	$363.00	$363.00
CREDIT CARD	$107.00	$107.00
CABLE/INTERNET	$125.00	$127.87
AUTO INSURANCE	$234.52	$324.52
PRE-SCHOOL	$800.00	$800.00
LIFE INSURANCE	$300.00	$300.00
VACATION FUND	$30.00	$102.00
CHURCH OFFERING	$25.00	$25.00
CHARITY	$63.00	$63.00
WATER BILL	$100.00	$100.00
LAWN SERVICE	$30.00	$30.00

FOR MORE EXAMPLES PLEASE VISIT WWW.HARRISADVISORSONLINE.COM

DECLARATION

I will maintain focus on my heavenly mountain climbing mission as I spend my money!

MOUNTAIN CLIMBING STEPS

21. How will you track your financial status? (Feel free to use the budget and balance sheet docs on the previous pages and also available on our website: www.mountainclimbingmoney.com.)

22. What are the obstacles you face when you consider maintaining your budget and financial scorecard?

23. Select an advisor, coach, or friend to act as an accountability partner. Select someone who understands and supports your mission.

CHAPTER 7

CONTINGENCY AND INSURANCE PLANNING

Murphy's Law happens—and it always seems to show up at the most inconvenient times. Contingency planning is about preparing for the worst case scenario. It's about preparing for that moment when what could go wrong does go wrong. What if you become disabled? What if you die prematurely? How does that affect your family? What happens to your spouse, kids, and family legacy? Will your family and those you trust most be able to handle your affairs if you're unable? The importance of contingency planning is often overlooked, because we have a natural tendency to avoid these and other questions that invoke more fear than hope. To address them effectively, we must face the uncertainty of the future and the facade of control we sometimes feel. However, the peace that can be found by addressing these issues will place us in a position of power to effectively move forward in life with confidence, knowing we have a firm foundation to stand on.

Some reading this will say, "God is my foundation." I agree with my whole heart. However, this fact is not to be used as justification for negligence. Paul told Timothy in First Timothy 5:8, "But if anyone does not provide for his own, and especially for those of his household, he has denied the faith and is worse than an unbeliever" (NKJV). Don't be naive and allow religious nonsense to rob you and your family of the blessing of protection. You will be able to withstand the troubles that come with life more confidently, and God will reward you with a greater abundance if you handle these matters effectively.

Balance is the key to effectively planning for this uncertainty. It often takes a lot of strategic planning to do this properly, so do the necessary work to strike that balance and prioritize your resources. Work with a professional who shares your perspective. As a novice, you do not want to attempt to understand all of the fine print on your own.

CASH RESERVES

Cash is king! Having a "rainy day" fund is a necessity. You should have anywhere from three to six months of cash in a savings account of some sort that is reserved strictly for absorbing the initial shock of the unforeseen. Depending on the circumstances, you may need more, but I'll address that later, when we discuss resource alignment. The important aspect of cash reserves is that it's immediately available. It's not going to grow much. Rates on savings accounts are essentially indexed to inflation, and on average you should expect your bank to pay around 1–1.5 percent below the current inflation rate. There is some variation to this, depending on the bank's business model. Online banks often pay higher rates, because they don't have the additional cost of brick and mortar. Research them though, because they may or may not provide FDIC coverage or immediate access. Be sure you understand the details of how the account works.

FDIC, in my opinion, is not as relevant as it was upon creation. The Federal Deposit Insurance Corporation was created by the Banking Act of 1933 in response to the collapse of the banking system in the great depression. There was no protection for customers of failed banks, and it became a spiraling situation as bank runs and failed loans drove more and more banks into default. The FDIC was created, among other institutions over the years, in an effort to provide confidence to consumers that the federal government would not allow another catastrophe akin to the failure in the great depression.

This is a very different consideration today. For instance, the federal government, in one form or another, injected over 4 trillion dollars into the financial system. The merits and effectiveness of this cash injection can be argued from many different angles; however, this did not involve the FDIC. The FDIC has been used as a means to facilitate the liquidation of failed institutions much more so than to protect consumers. One job of the FDIC is to act as a regulator, so in that instance there is some protection. However, that has not involved the insurance policy except in a few instances.

LIFE INSURANCE

How much life insurance is enough? What type of insurance should I have? These are two questions with an enormous amount of importance. I have included a worksheet that will allow you to evaluate the first question with a high degree of accuracy. But let me explain a couple of concepts before you jump in. Keep in mind that the types of insurance, the length of the term policy, and other important factors are too in depth and ultimately need to be evaluated for each individual's needs. Because of this, I'm unable to address every important factor in many of these decisions. Please find a trustworthy professional who can take the time to ensure your family will be aptly protected.

Life insurance is a vehicle that ultimately can be used to replace income in the event of a premature death. You are planning on saving, building a business, paying for college, leaving a legacy, and whatever other aspirations you may have. First and foremost, you must understand that you are not insuring your future hopes. You may see yourself as a multi-millionaire. However, currently you may only be living on $50,000 a year. Ensure that your family will be able to afford your current lifestyle for now. You don't want to have too much insurance; otherwise, you will be using resources that could be applied toward your future goals and purpose in the Kingdom.

The strategy *buy term and invest the difference* is often the best path when you're in the early stages of wealth-building and career/purpose development. Nonetheless, you must have *enough*. Use the included tool to enter your current budget, which should involve basic savings for financial independence (some say retirement) for your spouse, education for kids, and other basic goals that are of the highest priority to you and your family. This will then allow you to calculate how much, if any, additional insurance you will need beyond what you can provide from your employer sponsored benefits. Employer sponsored benefits will always be the most cost effective by maximizing what is allowed. However, if you're planning on leaving your employer in the near future, you should explore what you can get outside of your benefits, as those benefits will end with your employment. You can maintain your coverage through your employer once you leave; however, it will be much more expensive than what you could attain outside your employer.

Don't trust rules of thumb. There are plenty of assumptions that can be made, like saying you should have ten times your current income as a death benefit in life insurance. However, that's a great way to leave a disaster for your family. Don't trust that! Use the tool I've provided to ensure you have aptly prepared for what would most likely be the most tragic experience your family would ever face. I've seen too many times when a spouse is left with a few hundred thousand dollars, which at face value seems like a lot, but the spouse must also make dramatic life-changing decisions and face the emotional and psychological trauma of losing a spouse. That's a recipe for disaster, and no one should be forced to make those decisions.

Life insurance proceeds are not taxable! Keep that in mind when you're discussing your options. The proceeds can be invested and used to supplement income, which is one of the goals of this type of protection. Be careful that you don't make rash decisions and that you have a plan of action in the event of a tragedy. You should have a conservative assumption of the potential return you could realize from an appropriate investment strategy. This will put you in a place of preparedness so that you don't make hasty decisions if that day arises that you may regret later.

Your expenses *may* be reduced if a spouse is no longer with you, so speak openly and honestly about the lifestyle the remaining spouse would be comfortable with. Paying off the house is not enough! Maintaining the house, taxes, savings, education, and so forth will still be costly endeavors, which is why you should address these issues and revisit them periodically. I suggest you take a fresh look at these considerations at each life changing event, or at least every five years. A new child or other changes to your lifestyle or income will alter the needs of your cash flow and will, therefore, change the amount of life insurance coverage you require, so plan accordingly.

Single people may also need insurance sometimes. If you have anyone in your life that is counting on your income for their well-being, factor that in. Paying off your personal debt should not be considered, however. Your car can be turned back in. Your house can be handed over to the bank. Credit cards get written off. The bottom line is, if you're single and not responsible for anyone else, your life insurance needs will be very limited if not zero. Your family will never be responsible to pay off your debts if there's no money left, so don't leave a gift to the bank.

Also, consider your legacy when planning your life insurance needs. If you have children and want them to have an opportunity to go to college, start a business, or just generally pursue their passions and purpose when they have grown, even in the event of your premature death, you must think prudently about the amount of money required today to fund that future amount at an appropriate age. In a later chapter, I will discuss estate and legacy planning. The important note here is that you need to allow for a present dollar amount that, if invested properly, could provide for that legacy. I've also included a tool that makes that calculation a little easier.

Accidental death and dismemberment insurance (AD&D) is not life insurance! This will only provide a payout in very unique situations, so if you can get regular life insurance, do it. It will cost more than AD&D, but the coverage is real. If you die, aside from specific situations that don't apply to most people, it pays the benefit. The situations that negate life insurance are suicide in the first two years or active duty military. If you are active duty military, you can obtain coverage through appropriate channels. If you contemplate suicide, seek professional guidance and find the appropriate support to work through your troubles. Get set free from that, and you'll be fine.

LIFE INSURANCE CALCULATOR

INCOME

DESCRIPTION	PROJECTED INCOME FOR THE MONTH
REMAINING TAKE HOME PAY	$2000.00
TOTAL	$2000.00

LIFE INSURANCE

CURRENT INSURANCE	DEATH BENEFIT	ASSUMED RETURN	INFLATION ADJUSTED RETURN	PROJECTED MONTHLY INCOME
GROUP LIFE	$250,000.00	6%	3.41%	$711.83
TERM LIFE	$0.00	6%	3.41%	$0.00
		6%	3.41%	$0.00
		6%	3.41%	$0.00
PROJECTED MONTHLY INCOME				$711.83
RESULTING INCOME				-$2799.62

BUDGET

DESCRIPTION	PROJECTED
OFFERING/TITHE	-$500.00
SAVINGS	-$500.00
MORTGAGE/HOUSING	-$1200.00
CELL PHONE	-$100.00
CAR LOAN	-$250.00
GAS/ELECTRIC	-$120.00
FOOD	-$400.00
CABLE/INTERNET	-$100.00
AUTO GAS	-$300.00
MEDICAL	-$250.00
DAYCARE	-$500.00
WATER BILL	-$30.00
LAWN SERVICE	-$100.00
ENTERTAINMENT	-$100.00
TRAVEL	-$200.00
MISC	-$761.00
TOTAL	$5,511.00

LIFE INSURANCE DEFICIT

DB	NEEDED	ASSUMED %	IAR
GET IT!!	-$983,865.71	6%	3.41%

DISABILITY INSURANCE

As of 2013, over 39 million Americans were living with a disability, according to the U.S. Census Bureau. That's 12.6 percent of the population of the United States. Your income is of critical importance to your wellbeing. Even being single, if you become disabled, who will care for you and your expenses? Will they have ample resources to provide? Do you want to be a burden to your family, who will no doubt, if willing, be required to make dramatic changes to their lifestyle, even if there's enough money? I hope that is not your intention, and if you're reading this, I must assume you are not so selfish as to say, "They'll deal with it."

Once again, most companies provide a degree of long-term disability, and some even provide short-term disability. Long-term disability will usually begin after 90 days or longer of disability and up to one year. Typically, they will provide income until the age of 65 or until you are able to return to employment. However, your company benefits are integrated with social security, and therefore, an application for social security disability is required. Your benefits will be frozen until you receive disabled status from the Social Security Administration, which could take up to two years or longer. Sometimes this even involves hiring an attorney to fight on your behalf, which can be a costly endeavor in and of itself. This is an important consideration as you work to find balance between using your cash to prepare for tragedy and still prepare for your future goals. Short-term disability will cover the initial phase of a disability with typically a very short waiting period of maybe a week or a month. Sick days and vacation time can be used to cover that gap if it's available, but then ultimately cash is king.

Private insurance can be obtained to provide additional or replacement coverage. Private disability coverage is not taxable, so you do not need to replace 100 percent of your current income. The general rule here is that if you're paying the premium with money that's already been taxed, the benefit will not be. Therefore, that rule applies to employer sponsored plans in some cases as well.

Be careful that you don't purchase insurance that only applies to certain illnesses, thinking it applies to all disabilities. True disability coverage will apply, no matter the situation, if you're unable to work. The amount of insurance necessary will once again be obtained by looking at your current budget, factoring in some modest reductions typically, and then providing enough insurance.

DECLARATION

I will protect my house from the storms that come and build my resources as a firm foundation!

MOUNTAIN CLIMBING STEPS

24. How much cash reserves should you have? (Three times your monthly expenses is a minimum goal.)

25. How much life insurance should you have? (Anyone else who contributes toward your household expenses, like your spouse, should answer that as well.)

26. What would your life be like if you didn't have enough insurance? (This should also include your spouse.)

CHAPTER 8

INVESTMENT PLANNING

Each of these topics is incredibly complex, and this one is more so than all the others. Here, I will demonstrate some of the common tools and principles used in developing an investment plan. Keep in mind that as an entrepreneur you may be looking at a capital investment in your business as an investment. As an individual, you may be looking at purchasing a home or rental property as an investment. Whatever the circumstance, the economics and business case for the decision need to be understood and considered in the proper context. What I mean by context is important to explain.

ECONOMICS

You see, if you're planting a garden in Michigan (where I'm from), it's very important that the seeds be planted in the right season. The day within the season can be important, but ultimately the season is the most critical consideration. You see, if you select the best tomato seeds from the finest nursery, purchase topnotch fertilizer and gardening tools, study the perfect distribution ratio of those seeds so that they have the optimal opportunity for nutritional distribution and growth, and then plant in February, you will have *zero* harvest. On occasion, we have sunny 60-degree days in February, but looks can be deceiving. That "indian summer," as we call it, will kill your harvest before there's a single root in the ground.

Likewise, not only is the economic season important, but also the season of your life. I won't get into this too much, but investing all your cash and then suddenly realizing that you need new tires or that the insurance payment is due will cause you to rip your seeds out of the ground, and some will be lost in the process. Learn to take prudent risks that you understand. It pays to have your financial house in order.

The seasonal element to investment planning is primarily driven by the economic cycle, or as some refer to it, the business cycle. In Michigan, spring, summer, fall, and winter occur every year. They're beautiful in their own right, and diehard Michiganders love the changes in seasons. That is, until January and February, when we're all tired of gray skies and cold weather. There's a saying in Michigan, "If you don't like the weather, just wait." One of my favorite aspects of the changing seasons is that you have a general sense of what's coming next. When I see leaves turning brown and falling from the trees, it means I need to run to the store and pick up a winter coat for my son. He's growing fast and, therefore, won't be able to wear the one I bought him last year. It may still be 60–70 degrees, but if I procrastinate, all of the coats will be gone. We all know what comes next—cold and snow, pure and simple. Every year the cycle continues; only the intensity of the seasons changes.

In Michigan, as a result of the dramatic changes in temperature, we have a very diverse wardrobe. We have incredibly thick winter coats, hats, and gloves to withstand what may turn out to be a brutal winter. We also have a lot of shorts and t-shirts for the 90-degree days of July and August. Again, the question isn't whether summer will show up, only how many 90-degree days will come with it. The same is true of winter. Winter isn't bad, as I understand it scientifically. It creates an opportunity of cleansing and restoration for the soil, which is probably why there's a lot of produce grown in Michigan. We even have a wine industry in northern Michigan that is quietly becoming more and more popular.

Economics is a changing cycle as well. There are, therefore, changes that should be made to your investment strategies based on what season we are in. The economic cycle also needs to be the lens you see current data through. A 60-degree day in August is viewed differently than a 60-degree day in February. That's where I think most pundits and commentators on the economy get it wrong. There's a context to the data. If you simply look at data, you may become overly excited or depressingly fearful. Neither may be appropriate.

TODAY

Currently, we are in a growth phase of the economic cycle here in the United States. It's not pretty though. A lot of Americans have given up on job pursuits. College tuition and trade school tuition have soared, partly due to the increased demand of workers transforming their careers. According to the Bureau of Labor Statistics (BLS), as of July, 2015, 93 million Americans were not even trying to find a job. That number is the most disturbing I see. It's a number that has been consistently growing, partly due to the onslaught of baby boomers that are retiring, but largely due to a lack of optimism about job prospects.

In July 2015, approximately 843,000 Americans left their jobs and 826,000 were new entries to the job market. There were also 2.4 million that reentered the job search. This tells me that retirees aren't moving that needle much. We need to create the opportunity for college and high school graduates to pursue a worthwhile career. We also need context regarding the media onslaught of negativity. They are selling fear, and business is good. Turn it off if you have to. The media complains that the economy isn't growing at 5–6 percent, but I guarantee that if it was they would be talking about inflation fears and how the economy is growing too fast. There would be some fantastic story about how America's demise is just around the corner as a result of bubbles created from the "overheating" economy.

China is in trouble! Their economic activity is slowing, their currency is appreciating, and the communist party is doing everything to attempt to save face. Yes, it's true that they have 1.7 trillion U.S. dollars in the form of currency and treasury bonds. They are the largest foreign lender. However, the total U.S. federal debt is approximately 18 trillion, and therefore, the debt to China represents a small percentage of our overall debt. Also, there are fears that China will begin to liquidate their U.S. holdings and send the dollar plummeting. This is valid; however, in light of their current circumstances, it would be devastating to their economy and currency just as well. Their currency, the renminbi, moves in sync with our U.S. dollar. Therefore, if our currency falls apart, so will theirs. Also, the pundits are assuming our government would do nothing in return.

However, we don't have to sit on the sidelines. If we shut off the U.S. consumer base from China, it would obliterate their economy. We represent almost 20 percent of their economic output. If we add to that our allies in Europe, they would be in serious trouble. My point is, we need to make some serious changes to our fiscal policy and get government spending under control. The fear of China needs to be directed into meaningful negotiations within our government to address that issue and avoid what *could* happen much farther down the road. This issue is not a concern today though, and if our government thinks progressively, it can be resolved within a few years, and we can sever our bonds to them.

Don't forget Y2K! I remember walking into Home Depot prior to the turn of the new millennium and seeing generators lined up at the checkout lines. With tremendous foresight, however, an enormous sign on the facing wall read, "GENERATORS ARE NOT RETURNABLE." I was eagerly anticipating the stories that would surface from the media about how wrong they were. They are so arrogant! The public lets them get away with this manipulation, and they know it. Swine flu, Y2K, economic collapse, Snow-Mageddon, the next worse hay fever season ever—according to the media, the end of the world is always just around the corner. When one story fails, they have an exciting story to justify the next theory. My goal is to help you have context so you can see behind the veil of negativity (not unlike in the movie *The Matrix*) that the media has convinced many of us to accept.

INVESTMENT VEHICLES

To that end, there are two basic investment asset classes—equity and debt. Companies use the issuance of stock (equity) and bonds (debt) in an effort to raise money for various reasons. Governments also use bonds to raise money; however, because government is essentially "owned" by the public, they have no stock to issue. Raising capital is the purpose of the issuer, and this is true if you are buying individual securities, mutual funds, a form of insurance, and so forth. Asset classes are then broken up into U.S. and international; then they are divided by categories into large, mid, small-cap, and growth or value on the equity side. On the debt side, bonds are separated by whether they are U.S. or international and then by credit rating. I will focus on bonds first.

BONDS

Bonds are debts owed that, in most cases, result in streams of income. Bond performance is primarily driven by that income known as interest. The price of the bond, which is issued at par value (typically $100) divided by the income stream is known as the yield on that bond. There are forms of bonds called zero-coupon bonds that do not pay interest. I will not be addressing those here, as they are not as common. The price of bonds moves with changes in interest rates. Changes in rates have a measure of impact on a bond, which is known as duration. Credit ratings are the credit score of corporations and governments. The higher the score, the less risk and, therefore, the lower the impact that changes in rates will often have. Duration is represented below.

We are in a season when rates are beginning to rise and a gradual increase in rates is expected over the next several years. That makes bond purchases of any kind a sensitive subject, and they should be made with all diligence and a degree of reservation.

International bonds are often denominated in foreign currencies. As a result of this, the consideration of currency exchange is critical. If a foreign government were to devalue their currency (as most are doing today), it would cause the value of a bond denominated in that currency to decline to a U.S.-based investor without any adverse actions of the corporation that issued it. This result is due to the fact that the interest paid from that bond is not worth as much here in the U.S., based on the declining currency exchange, and therefore, the bond itself is not as valuable to U.S. investors.

Bonds are guaranteed streams of income, with the return of principle typically happening at maturity. There are many forms, but this is the most common. It is important to note that this "guarantee" of the return of your initial investment only applies to individual bonds. Buying mutual funds or other investment vehicles that invest in bonds will not provide the same guarantee. In most cases, there is no guarantee whatsoever. In some cases, there are other features of the account that may appear as a guaranteed return of principle or performance. Be careful and be certain to understand the limitations of such returns.

STOCKS

A stock is a security that carries with it a degree of ownership in a publicly traded company. A company like Apple issues shares for the purpose of raising capital. There is a board of directors that then votes on dividends paid out to shareholders and any changes to the fractional share ownership represented by the stock. Splits, for instance, are voted on by the board, which is there to act as fiduciaries along with senior management of public money (in the form of stock ownership).

It is important to understand that the stock is not the company, and the company is not the stock. What I mean is that the stock may not perform well, even though the company is making record profits, and vice versa. Many investors have challenges with grasping this dynamic. For instance, during the last recession, I had a conversation with an investor who had purchased shares of General Motors despite my advice. It was the spring of 2008, and we were in a recession. During that particular recession, GM was faced with insurmountable challenges and was running out of options. They were ultimately faced with a federally directed bankruptcy. This caused the stock to be dismissed, reducing its value to $0.

I had several unfortunate conversations with this client, who could not grasp that GM would continue making cars while the stock value would be reduced to nothing. He, despite my strong efforts to educate and persuade him, lost the entire amount of his investment. He kept saying, "Let's just see what happens. I think they'll be OK." He was unable to see that the stock is not the company, and despite GM still making cars today, the stock at the time became worthless. GM subsequently issued new shares of the restructured company and is still making cars today.

The S&P 500 and Dow Jones Industrial average are the two most widely known indexes that act as benchmarks for the stock performance of large U.S.-based corporations. These indexes are a representation of large cap stocks, or as they are commonly referred to, "blue chip stocks." A stock may perform differently than the index for better or worse. Market capitalization (market cap) is how you measure the size or value of the stock itself. It's important to note that the assets of the company may, and usually will, differ from the value of the stock. Market cap is determined by taking the number of outstanding shares of the corporation and multiplying by the current share price.

100 Million shares x $10/share price = Market cap of $1 Billion

Large cap stocks are stocks with a market cap of at least $10 billion. Mid cap are stocks with a market cap of between $2 billion and $10 billion, while the market cap of small cap stocks may vary, but is generally from $300 million to $2 billion. Typically, the smaller the market cap on a stock, the more volatile it will be on a daily basis.

Stock prices move any time the market is open, which in New York is from 9:30 a.m. to 4 p.m. Eastern Standard Time. Holidays affect market opening, and of course, different exchanges open at different times around the world. After-hours trading, however, is available at some brokerage firms. There are potentially additional considerations with after-hours trading that are a bit advanced for the purpose of this book and should not be taken lightly.

Stock prices are quoted with a bid price, ask price, and recent trade price. The bid price is a notification of the last offer to buy that particular stock. The ask is notification of the last offer to sell. There are also many types of orders that can be used to perform a stock purchase or sell, which can vary depending on the brokerage company you're using. The terminology can also vary. You should become familiar with these options at your firm of choice, as it can dramatically affect the performance of your particular transaction.

Stocks are evaluated on a number of different points. I won't be going into detail here on the many different points. However, two of the primary approaches are fundamental analysis and technical analysis.

Fundamental analysis is the consideration of the performance of the underlying company as it relates to the price per share of the stock. Is the company profitable compared to its peers? Is the stock priced higher or lower in reference to earnings among its peers? Does the company have prospects of increasing earnings moving forward? Ultimately, is the stock priced at a point that makes it attractive compared to other available options? There are a number of different considerations when evaluating a stock from this perspective. Many investors have had a tremendous amount of success evaluating stocks using this approach. Warren Buffet is one of them. Fundamental analysis is the oldest and most widely used approach to investment evaluation; however, others swear by technical analysis.

Technical analysis is driven by evaluating the movements of the price of the stock by the use of charts. Degrees of movements tell technical investors what to expect from the price of the stock. Pure technical analysis makes no consideration of the performance of the underlying company. It may be a disaster driven by poor management and horrible financials. If the chart looks good they like it, if not they don't.

FUNDS

Investment companies realized they could make money by giving investors the opportunity to pool their resources and then providing those investors with ongoing investment advice and management. The most common forms of this structure are mutual funds and exchange traded funds. Mutual funds are only transacted at the close of a trading day, while exchange traded funds trade throughout market hours like a stock. The important thing to understand is that funds are not aggressive or conservative; they can be across the risk spectrum, depending on the investment strategy they employ. They will generally perform according to the assets they invest in, which could include just about anything. This information will never be completely transparent and will only be understood by reviewing and understanding the guidelines contained in the related prospectus for that fund. These funds may invest in stocks, bonds, precious metals, real estate, or almost any asset in any combination. All of that will be detailed in the prospectus.

For many, the benefit of mutual funds or exchange traded funds is that they alleviate issuer risk. For example, if I have $100,000 and use the entire amount to invest in Microsoft, I am not diversified, and therefore, I am subject to issuer risk. All my eggs are in one basket, so if the basket tips, breaks, or gets stepped on, I'm in big trouble. If Microsoft then runs into problems, whether it is a bad headline or bankruptcy, then my full investment will be at the mercy of that one company. One way to diversify is to invest in many different stocks. If Microsoft only represents 5 percent of my overall investment, then the results of that one stock will not result in a dramatic sway on my total investment. However, stocks are all on the same road.

If I line up a Ford Mustang, a Cadillac sedan, a pick-up truck, and an SUV on a winding road, they will all turn at the same time. The only difference is the experience of the driver. Stocks are like that, generally speaking. When economic times are good, stocks do well. When we're moving into a recession, stocks perform badly. When people tell me they have "conservative stocks," I tell them that's like telling me they have a friendly grizzly bear they want me to meet. Sorry, but I don't think so! I'm all for taking risk, but don't try to pretend a bear is a teddy if it isn't. Global and domestic economic changes will cause stocks to change direction. It's important to understand how what you're investing in will respond and to what degree. Make sure you understand the good, the bad, and the ugly before making investment decisions. Though funds can help diversify your investment, they involve risk, and it is important that you are fully aware of that risk.

There are many more ways to invest in the same assets I have outlined above. I could go on and on, but my goal here is not to bore you with all of the ways you could invest. Rather, I have given you a simple window into the inner workings of the most commonly used and discussed types of investments. Be certain to get professional advice from someone you trust to assist you with investment decisions and who shares your perspective on your journey.

DECLARATION

I make investment decisions prudently, understanding the return and potential risks associated with every decision.

MOUNTAIN CLIMBING STEPS

It's OK if you've never invested. Just skip the next three steps and keep going.

27. Check your investment account performance daily for the next 21 days. Take note of any emotions that arise.

28. What is the worst investment decision you have ever made?

29. What is the best investment decision you have ever made?

CHAPTER 9

GOAL PLANNING

Alan Lakein, well-known author on the subject of time management, has said, "Planning is bringing the future into the present so that you can do something about it now." For many of us, retirement is one of the biggest goals we plan toward. The concept of retirement began in the late 1800s, pioneered in Germany by a man named Otto von Bismarck. He eventually created the first government pension, which was the model for what is now social security. The idea was that the government should provide for those who were too old to work. He stated, "Those who are disabled from work by age and invalidity have a well-grounded claim to care from the state." The word *invalidity* carries a powerful underlying message, suggesting that in old age you are invalid to society. Do you want to see yourself as invalid? Does God view you as irrelevant in your later years? I say *no!*

Even though retirement isn't the only goal many are preparing for, it is often the biggest. Instead, I believe financial independence should be the bulls-eye we are aiming for, not retirement. The result may look similar, but the context and perspective are very different.

Imagine that you're a farmer reaping your hard-earned harvest. You prepared your field with arduous effort. You planted your seeds, and with care you saw it grow. Now it's time to reap the results of your labor. After tabulating your results, you find that you have achieved a stellar crop. You have farmed for years. Through trial and error and diligent effort, you have acquired a set of skills it takes a lifetime to earn. However, this year has been challenging because you are moving a little slower than in the past, and the amount of effort required to complete the tasks continues to increase each year. Your knowledge, however, is irreplaceable. Do you halt your endeavors, seeing that you have amassed a self-sustainable wealth? Do you give in to the realization that you may not desire to continue to work? Is it too hard now to continue your pursuits? Perhaps you should just change your perspective.

God has given you a goal, a vision. The clearer you can articulate that vision, the more aggressively you can pursue it. If you are on a dark path with limited perception of the path in front of you, then the speed and aggression with which you traverse that path will also be limited. The children of Israel found themselves chasing their own tails in a circle for forty years because they couldn't see the path into the promised land that God had showed them long ago. They were overwhelmed by what seemed to be an unconquerable foe. All the while, God was looking at grasshoppers.

You have a distinct blueprint in front of you that God has placed in your heart, and money is required to make it a reality. Financial independence is one cog in the wheel of the vision God has for you. Money provides independence, options, and freedom. It gives you the freedom to aggressively pursue the rebuilding of that wall, the independence to save a nation. Money opens doors. Some people are at a place where their first goal is to pay next month's bills. Others are pursuing expansive career options in politics or their next business venture. No matter what the goal may be, financial independence provides the key to opening the door to it.

Now that we're all focused on financial independence alongside whatever pursuits God has burning in our hearts, let's talk about the considerations we need to understand to bring focus to our financial decisions. The key is that we are not focused on a return or the childish pursuit of selfishness. Instead, we need to know how to plant our seeds according to the fruit, or circumstances, we want to produce with them. The way we do this is by understanding liquidity.

LIQUIDITY

Having access to money at the right time without being encumbered by penalties or tax burdens is critical. I encourage clients to separate financial decisions into three time frames; 0–3 years, 3–7 years, and 7+ years. Your personal circumstances and the global, domestic, and local economic environment must have a large influence on the timing of your decisions, as well as the placement of your resources.

0–3 YEARS

Here the focus is on short-term, if not immediate, access. Fluctuation in principle is not acceptable in most cases here. You must also accept that your return will be minimal and will most likely not keep up with inflation. This is part of the plan. I have seen people not heed my advice and find themselves forced to delay their life-long dreams as a result of this matter. Don't be overly optimistic. Rather, allow prudence to be your guide. Often, bank accounts are the best choice for this portion of your resources. You may be able to boost your return slightly by using a certificate of deposit or an online bank account. Stay away from anything that does not carry full protection of your principle or that ties your money up for longer than your planned use. Also, annuities don't work here, as you'll see later. They carry a tax problem that, if not understood, will deteriorate your ability to execute your plan.

3-7 YEARS

Our liquidity needs are much less here, and a modest degree of speculation and volatility may be acceptable, depending on the market and economic environment. Stay away from tax deferred accounts unless you're over 59 ½ years old, or you will find yourself paying a 10 percent excise tax on your withdrawals. Even still, I prefer a taxable account or municipal bonds here, because the short-term nature of these objectives favors flexibility. Using a tax deferred account may result in minimal tax savings, and other unforeseen negative consequences may cause you to be forced off course. It is not worth the risk. A keen understanding of the underlying market and economic environment is critical here. You don't want to throw good money into a bad market. For example, investing in the stock market at the end of 2007 with funds needed in the three to seven year time frame would not have been a good decision. In the right environment, either bonds, stocks, or mutual funds could make sense, depending on how comfortable you are with short-term volatility.

7+ YEARS

In this third time frame, you have time on your side. Depending on your age, you may be able to be a bit more aggressive or also pursue some tax advantages, which I will address in the next chapter. In a growth phase in the economic cycle, you should be as aggressive as your heart desires. Don't be foolish though. Refrain from running out and just buying investment vehicles. Have a clear investment strategy that is tailored to the current and coming economic environment. This is counter to what the general financial industry will tell you. They will tell you to devote your resources to "good" investments. I don't believe there's such a thing. The only good investment is the one that's good for you, based on current economic conditions. Funds, annuities, stocks, bonds, and bank accounts are all appropriate considerations. Even real estate may be a consideration, depending on your goals. The key here is to focus on your purpose, keeping the economic conditions in the forefront of your thought process. From there, plant your seeds with care and see your harvest develop.

It has often been said, "If you aim at nothing you are sure to hit it." I have seen this play out countless times while helping clients make financial decisions. Too often, the elderly die, leaving fortunes, while their families and countless causes could have found wonderful uses for their resources—if only they had intentionally planned how to use them. If you have ample resources, you may simply need to clarify your purpose and then align your resources accordingly. Don't hesitate! Of course, even if you do not yet have a large amount of resources, you should not look at your bank account and say, "I'm behind," or, "Why bother?" Let go of every doubt, insecurity, and past mistake. Rather, press on with intentionality. Accept where you are, and move forward with purposeful decisions. If you're reading this, you are on the right track. Now take the truth you've been armed with, and fight the good fight.

DECLARATION

I will make financial decisions with a keen focus on my heavenly mission and the financial well being of myself and my family!

MOUNTAIN CLIMBING STEPS

30. On a scale of 1–10 how do you rate your progress toward your goals? (1 = not on track at all, 10 = 100 percent on track)

31. What strategies can you utilize to reduce your tax liability?

32. Are you investing in a manner that provides flexibility for you to adapt as you gain insight into your mountain climbing mission?

CHAPTER 10

TAX PLANNING

As mentioned previously, diversification is critically important when making financial decisions or plans. Having diversity in a portfolio of stocks, mutual funds, and such reduces or nearly eliminates certain types of risk. In a business, diversification will often provide resiliency during changing economic environments. If your sole business is to sell umbrellas and you live in a place where it never rains, your business model may need some work. Also, if your biggest client is 80 percent of your revenue, and then that particular client runs into trouble, you may find yourself wondering how payroll will be met. As these examples show, diversification in assets or income streams is crucial. Likewise, tax diversification should be a significant consideration in financial planning. Tax planning, as it relates to this discussion, is a matter of giving the IRS the least amount possible so that more can be applied to what's important to you. This translates into more being used for the Kingdom purposes at hand. Jesus said to render to Caesar what is Caesar's, but I would add, don't give more than you must.

Tax diversification may be a new concept to many, but whether you're hoping to start a business or buy a house, are in a time of transition, or are looking at expanding your business operations, it is a tremendous tool that will provide you with strategic choices you would not have otherwise.

THREE PRIMARY ENVIRONMENTS

There are three primary tax environments for an individual with cash to invest in an account—taxable, pre-tax deferred, and after-tax untaxed. (If you're a business owner looking to invest in equipment or assets relating to your business, there are different considerations that I won't be addressing here.)

Of these three, taxable accounts are the most common. If you have a bank account, you are familiar with this concept. You have money you received in your paycheck that has already been taxed as income. That then gets deposited into your bank account to pay bills and such. That financial institution will then send you a 1099-INT at tax time, where it will report whatever interest you received on that account for the previous year. That interest is then reported on your 1040 tax return and is taxable as income for the year you received the interest. Basically, you pay taxes as you go on this account. Non-retirement investment accounts usually fall in this category as well. Dividends and capital gains from stocks, bonds, and funds will also be taxable in the year the return is realized. If you buy an investment that grows, but you do not sell it, then you have not yet *realized* the appreciation, and it is, therefore, not taxable. That is referred to as *unrealized gains.* This is important, because you can use a realized loss to offset a realized gain, so you can strategically reallocate assets when appropriate and reduce your tax consequences.

A 401k, 403b, IRA, and so forth are all examples of pre-tax tax deferred accounts. The contributions placed into these accounts have not been taxed, or you will receive a deduction on your tax return for them. As the account grows, you will not be taxed on any return or your contribution until you receive money from these accounts. The key here are the restrictions. You do not have complete flexibility with these accounts until you are 59 ½ years old. Until then, you will receive a special excise tax penalty of 10 percent on any funds withdrawn from these accounts. You can take a loan on 401ks; however, this is quite possibly the worst transaction you could make on one of these accounts. You see, the money borrowed from a 401k is not taxed initially, but you pay taxes on the payments made back into the account. You then get the treat of paying taxes on the money all over again when you begin making withdrawals. In other words, you get to pay the IRA twice on the same dollar. If your tax rate is 20 percent, you just doubled it to 40 percent. This should be a last resort only!

There are a few special circumstances that allow withdrawals early, but essentially, you have to be swamped with medical bills to void the 10 percent excise tax penalty on withdrawals. The rule for required minimum distributions (RMD) is that at the age of 70 ½, whether you like it or not, you must make a minimum withdrawal on these accounts that is based on calculation the IRS has established, and you must pay taxes on that amount. It's like the old saying, "You don't have to go home, but you can't stay here." You don't have to spend the money, but you can't leave it in the account. One additional note on this tax environment: If you're over the age of 50 and you stop working a day job, you may be able to begin making withdrawals, known as systematic equal periodic payments. There is a maximum amount the IRS will allow in this circumstance, and it cannot be changed for five years or until the age of 59 ½, whichever is later. If you mess this up, you get socked pretty hard by the IRS, so be sure to seek help.

The after-tax non taxable environment is finicky. The reason I say this is because there are several ways to get into this environment. One is a Roth IRA. You contribute money into a Roth and never pay taxes on the growth so long as you play by the rules. The contribution you make can be withdrawn from the account for any reason after five years. The growth will never be taxed if you wait until you are 59 ½ or if you use it for college expenses. The interest on some municipal bonds is not taxed at the federal level, and if you live in the state of the municipality, you generally will not pay state taxes either, if applicable. Cash value life insurance can also fall into this group; however, it should only be considered if you're in one of the highest tax brackets or if you're in a career that carries high legal liability.

One quasi-environment that only applies to one account type is tax-deferred annuities. The premium you place in these accounts has already been taxed. It is not taxed until you make a withdrawal. However, instead of it being taxed as a potential capital gain, like a taxable account (typically 10 percent rate), you get to pay income taxes on the gains, which is typically much higher. You are also subject to the 59 ½ years of age rule on these accounts, so be careful. In my opinion, these should be used sparingly due to the higher tax rates. You also cannot take the taxed money out before the tax-deferred gains. The gains always come out first.

The key with this topic is that you should think strategically about the tax consequences when considering your goals. Don't get stuck having the money you need in the wrong tax environment. The best case scenario, if you find yourself in your mid-60s looking to generate a paycheck to fund the next stage of your life, is to have multiple tax environments to draw from so that you can influence your overall tax liability. Also, tax laws change and, therefore, tax diversification provides you the opportunity to adapt to those changes without being killed with unnecessary tax burdens. Obamacare has also tacked on an additional tax for those making too much money, so be aware of that. You get to pay additional taxes on all income (even non-taxable municipal bonds) if you make above $250,000 as a married couple.

In closing, it is important to note that business owners have the greatest flexibility. As a business owner, you can get creative with the right help, so start a business. Besides, entrepreneurialism is Kingdom building, so do it now!

DECLARATION

I am prudent to ensure I consider tax reduction strategies when at all possible.

MOUNTAIN CLIMBING STEPS

33. Identify a tax planning expert who can assist you in evaluating your tax reduction options (accountant, CPA, financial planner).

34. What is one strategy you can utilize immediately to reduce your overall tax liability?

35. Commit to reviewing the tax consequences of any major financial decision with a professional.

CHAPTER 11

LEGACY PLANNING

Proverbs 13:22 says, "A good man leaves an inheritance to his children's children, but the wealth of the sinner is stored up for the righteous" (NKJV). The message that will resound through the future annals of history is contained within this verse. It expands beyond our immediate family or our bloodline, which is of great importance. I have always aspired to live out the principle contained in this verse. However, I have begun to see legacy as so much more than I once did, in light of evaluating Kingdom-minded decisions.

I desire to build wealth, and I am in the process of creating an opportunity for my children and their children as I continue on my journey. Still, there's something far greater at stake. We are called to serve our generation as David did. I think inside us all is a desire to accomplish something that will last, to take new territories for the Kingdom and establish God's name as preeminent in the spheres we are called to. That propels us into our future and calls us to make sacrifices today. That is the driving force that compels us to look beyond our 401ks and investment accounts and to read books like this one.

Part of building a legacy is protecting it. Having the right legal structures can protect your assets from unnecessary fees, taxes, and overall costs that dramatically reduce the amount of resources available for your family, church, charities, and others to continue your life's endeavors when you're unable to continue them yourself.

These matters can become a daunting task to address, and depending on your financial picture, they can be cumbersome to sort through on your own. I'm going to address a few key components that apply to the general public, as well as touching on several other items that may be relevant, depending on your net worth. Let me interject a caveat: Each state has laws that may deviate slightly from some statements contained in this section. I will speak on some common ground; however, the nuances of your state laws need to be carefully considered by a professional. I can connect you with someone who can help you with this, if you like.

A WILL = PROBATE

A will, or what's commonly referred to as a living will, is a requested distribution schedule for your estate when you die. A will typically addresses guardianship when you have minor children as well. One goal you should have if you pass is to avoid probate for your assets. Probate can become a very costly and time-consuming process. What happens is, upon your passing, someone files a request with the probate court in the county of jurisdiction, which is typically based on your residency upon passing. If there is only one person filing that request, this is typically relatively simple. However, if there is a dispute over who should have this responsibility, this can become a severe complication, particularly if loved ones are waiting for your assets to pay bills and resume their lives.

After being appointed the legal representative of your estate, they are empowered to settle your estate and distribute the funds accordingly. Debtors are normally notified by a written notice in a local newspaper to give them an opportunity to file a claim on your estate. There is often a waiting period, when your assets are frozen, which can be six months or longer. If there is a claim, it must be heard, justified by documentation, and a settlement agreed upon before anyone gets paid.

A will can also be contested by anyone who feels they have a justified issue with the will or distribution schedule agreed upon by the probate court. This is where it can get ugly. Siblings, cousins, friends, and others can spring up out of the woodwork and, if nothing else, cause delays, attorney fees, court fees, and an overall pain in the butt for the personal representative of the deceased.

Probate can be a nasty, painful process and typically will consume 40 percent or more of an estate and will tie up your assets for two years. Protecting your assets from probate is not hard to do. You simply need to have beneficiaries on your accounts.

BENEFICIARY DESIGNATIONS

There are several versions of beneficiary designations. Payable on death, transfer on death, and beneficiary designations are all the same thing on different accounts and in different states.

Life insurance, annuities, and retirement accounts will always have the opportunity to have beneficiary designations. If you're married, it will require a signature from your spouse if you want someone other than your spouse to be designated the beneficiary of your retirement account. You can have a back up beneficiary on these accounts, in the event you and your spouse pass away in a car accident or plane accident. One key here is that you do not want a minor to be a beneficiary, because they will not be able to file a claim to receive the benefits of the account. There is an alternative structure, known as a revocable living trust, that often makes sense when minor children are involved.

Payable on death or transfer on death designations are applicable on non-IRA accounts. This can be an investment or bank account. In either of these situations, the money is immediately transferred to the beneficiary upon your death, and no probate or court proceeding is required. The beneficiary only needs to present a death certificate and fill out some paperwork to take ownership and control of your accounts. The paperwork can be a bit of a hassle, so a little help goes a long way in processing this efficiently.

Occasionally verify that your beneficiary designations are according to your wishes (at least every five years). You never know what you may have forgotten to correct. I've seen money go to the wrong people because a fax didn't go through or a box wasn't checked by someone who got a form in the mail. Use the old craftsman rule of measure twice and cut once. Verify, verify, verify! These cannot be disputed, so making sure they are set up according to your wishes is critical. Johnny can show up at your bank with that little note you wrote him every day for the next 12 years, but he's not getting a penny unless he's a beneficiary.

Each financial institution has its own guidelines for processing the claim, so keep that in mind when you consider how many institutions you're doing business with. How much running around do you want your widow to do? How much of a hassle do you want to put your family through? Most financial institutions can handle a lot of whatever products you might use, so consider consolidating for ease of use and convenience if all other things are equal.

TRUSTS

There are around 350 different types of trusts in existence today. The most common is the revocable living trust (RLT). This is the equivalent of creating a business of you. You create a legal entity that doesn't really exist until you die. After your passing, it gets its own tax ID and retains control of your assets based on your explicit wishes. You designate who runs the business after you're gone; however, there is a degree of accountability to ensure your wishes are carried out. If you're unable to make your own decisions, there are typically clauses in place that address this so that your successor trustee can step in and pay your bills and handle your affairs until you pass. Sometimes your incapacitation is addressed through a power of attorney (POA), which is important to understand. If you use a trust, it is important that your other documents, such as the POA, work in conjunction with your trust. I've seen folks who have a trust controlling all of their assets, but the attorney was a knuckle head who didn't address their incapacitation in their trust, and then—oops!—the POA doesn't apply to the trust, so now we have a problem.

A trust can retain control of your assets after you're gone. It can hold onto money for your minor children. It can protect money from a mess your family may find themselves in. It can provide income for a disabled family member or the care of the elderly. It will most likely contain a clause that eliminates the opportunity for your family to fight over who gets what. It can even provide for the continuation of a business if everything is set up right.

When I begin working with a client, one of the first things I want to see is their legal documents (trust, will, POA, HCPAD) to verify that we know how they work and to confirm they work the way the client thinks they work. It can be a mess sometimes, but usually if you work with an experienced estate planning attorney, you'll be OK. These documents also help me understand how to properly fund a person's trust so that the accounts are set up in alignment with these documents. I can't tell you how many times clients have thought those expensive documents solved all of their estate planning needs. They don't! Without properly aligning your accounts through a process known as "funding your trust," that document is nothing but an expensive use of a tree.

A trust, if properly funded, will avoid probate; however, you must keep in mind that so do beneficiary designations. A trust should be seriously considered if you have minor children, in the event that no remaining parent or guardian remains, or if a disability in the family would cause you to want control over distributions. If you're concerned your beneficiary may not be able or willing to do what's in their best interest, a revocable living trust (RLT) is the way to go.

A RLT will be helpful with blended families as well. If you are in a second marriage late in life, and you both have different views over what should happen upon your passing, you can use one trust or separate RLTs to carry out your wishes, so long as funding them has been completed properly.

Estate or "death" taxes can also be controlled to a degree using this tool. Currently, an individual can die with a net worth of 5.45 million dollars without any federal estate taxes. If the last man or woman standing is worth more than 5.45 million dollars, then the beneficiaries have estate taxes to pay. You can separate your assets among two separate RLTs to double that amount if necessary and pay no estate taxes. If your total net worth is over 6 million, this should be an important consideration. Each spouse can also have their own RLT; then you would split the assets around the middle to ensure you're taking advantage of this clause. Currently, the estate tax bracket begins at 18 percent and goes up to 40 percent on the amount above 5.45 million. If you're worth 10 million dollars, you can save almost 1.8 million dollars in tax liability by using this strategy. If you're net worth is above 10 million, you can get a lot more creative and still have a great reduction of your tax bill, but a high degree of specialization is required.

HEALTH CARE

Either a health care power of attorney or a patient advocate designation are used to empower someone you trust to make medical decisions for you if you're unable to make them yourself due to incapacitation. The important thing to look for is to ensure it is HIPAA compliant. The Health Insurance Privacy Act of America is a law that was passed several years ago and will be addressed by any respectable estate planning attorney. This document will also provide some direction to your family regarding end of life care like life support. Having things spelled out clearly often will help your family make difficult decisions, because you made the decision for them. They won't have to wrestle, trying to figure out what you want, if you spell it out for them, so do it.

This will also ensure that the person you select has the authority to make those decisions and communicate with your physicians. This can become a big deal if you're in a nursing home or a coma. If you're over the age of 18, your parents can't make medical decisions for you, so get these documents in place for your adult children also.

THOUGHT PROCESS

As you evaluate your legacy, think of things you want to accomplish through the end of your life. Don't just think about what you want to happen after you've left this world. Ensure your documents are written to fulfill your life's work or purpose. There's nothing wrong with having funds go to charities, churches, ministries, or even for-profit companies that align with your purpose. With careful consideration and planning, you can leave an opportunity for your family as well as funds to go toward your life's work. "It is appointed for man to die once..." (Heb. 9:27). Being prepared for that event shows that you take your calling seriously and provides a firm foundation for you to stand on, no matter when your day arrives.

DECLARATION

I will exercise great care in taking the necessary steps to protect my family and my mountain climbing mission.

MOUNTAIN CLIMBING STEPS

36. What steps have you taken to ensure your legal structures are in place for estate / legacy planning?

37. What three tasks would you want completed if you were unable to fulfill them due to illness or death?

38. Identify a legal or financial professional who supports your mission and who can review your documents to ensure they are in alignment with your priorities.

— PART 3 —

ALIGNING RESOURCES

In this final section of this book, I will deal with the unseen forces that drive your financial decisions and the understanding you must have if you are to successfully move forward to the next summit on your journey. Psychology and neuroscience have seen significant breakthroughs over the last several decades in identifying what's going on between our ears. As I have poured over psychology and personal development literature and attended numerous trainings on the matter, I've seen a shift in perspective from experts in the field. They are realizing that our mind is not our brain.

It's kind of humorous for me to be "out of my mind," but it's an interesting thought. You see, our brain is a series of electrical circuits, not thoughts and feelings. What we have learned is that our thought lives impact the circuits functioning in our brains, not the other way around. Our souls can prosper and then impact our physiology in the right direction. As Jesus says, "The lamp of the body is the eye. If therefore your eye is good, your whole body will be full of light. But if your eye is bad, your whole body will be full of darkness" (Matt. 6:22–23 NKJV). Science is beginning to catch up with the truth of Bible.

Emotional intelligence is a concept I have studied for about twenty years. The key pillars of emotional intelligence are personal responsibility, self-awareness, and sustained motivation. Those three areas are being identified as the most important components of individual development. You can grow in each of these areas and conquer the hardest and biggest mountain—*you!* I committed long ago, to God and to myself, that I would view my body as a living sacrifice, as a tool designed to glorify Christ. That includes my thoughts, emotions, decisions, relational skills, and every unseen aspect of my identity. That's not an easy commitment to make, and it's much harder to keep consistently. However, armed with the right knowledge and truth, I am much more fulfilled and fruitful in my activities. When I can take an honest look at my life and the results I'm producing, I can move forward boldly, making appropriate adjustments and moving confidently into the future.

Emotional intelligence and the underlying emotional quotient (EQ), which refers to your ability to excel at managing you, are singularly focused on you and your ability to manage yourself. From the place of self-mastery, you are then able to find the strength and skills necessary to excel in external situations. Relationships are critical in whatever arena you are pursuing. Having a high EQ brings you into a place of favor. You will manage your emotions and not become defensive or critical when confronted. You will also not cower to intimidation. Instead, you will stand tall on the principles and foundation of truth that your life is based upon.

The challenge we face is our subconscious. In his landmark book, *Thinking, Fast and Slow,* Dr. Daniel Kahneman describes how we have differing and often conflicting thought processes. The fast process is the responsive network of our subconscious, where in an instant we act or respond without thoughtful introspection or processing of information. This is often the most challenging for us, and it is where we have the most blind spots that restrain us from the glorious future Christ has placed in us. When Paul said we must be transformed by renewing our minds (see Rom. 12:2), I'm convinced he was speaking about both the fast and slow centers; however, the fast is often the most deceptive.

As human beings, we have around ten thousand words or messages surging in our subconscious every second of every day. It's like a rushing white river, and when those centers in our brains are triggered, we just jump in that stream and go for a ride, often taking those around us along. Mastery in this area is like being able to guide ourselves as we are moving so that anger does not turn into violence and fear does not turn into petrification or depression. The fast mental processes are not bad, of course. They also tell us to laugh at a joke or protect our family if necessary. Mastering this neural center is the critical piece.

The slow mental processes, according to Dr. Kahneman, are the calculating, planning centers of the brain and thought life. We need these processes to pay our bills and get our work done efficiently. Having these neural processes mastered is key to sustaining motivation, effectively completing projects, and not letting our friends down when making dinner plans. All work and no play makes Jack a dull boy, so both mental processes should be appreciated and developed, just like any other skill.

Here is the most critical component of climbing a cultural mountain for the Kingdom—you must wrestle with God. In doing so, you find yourself moving into submission to His will, as Jacob did while he was becoming Israel (see Gen. 32). The Holy Spirit will guide your hands and lead you into a path of all knowledge and truth, where you will find ample resources to produce a remarkable harvest of physical, spiritual, and supernatural fruit. God will guide you on your journey up the mountain, and you will find that as you progress in diligence and development, suddenly the desires of the past will become irrelevant and new passions will be paramount. I see it as ascending into Heaven. As you climb, the altitude will cause the pains and disappointments of the past to fall off. The very foundations of self-doubt and pity will deteriorate.

You must focus on your own development, self-awareness, discipline, and mission. As you do, God will continue to bless you with a confidence in His calling and gifts in your life. The resources of Heaven and earth will come into alignment as you go. Much of this next section speaks about conquering yourself so that you will then conquer your money and your mountain.

DECLARATION

I have command of my mind, body, and soul, and I choose to aggressively pursue my mountain climbing mission.

MOUNTAIN CLIMBING STEPS

39. Identify at least one occasion when you allowed your emotions to sway your financial decisions and it ended poorly.

40. Identify at least one occasion when you made a tough financial decision in dedication to a more important goal.

41. Identify an accountability partner who will challenge you to be your best in making financial decisions.

CHAPTER 12

A PROSPEROUS SOUL

The apostle John wrote to the early believers, "Beloved, I pray that you may prosper in all things and be in health, just as your soul prospers" (3 John 2 NKJV). This is a critical point, because the best education without the proper mindset will self-destruct. I have lived this out, and I have been witness to the destructive forces within us. We find an example of this in Tim Geitner, who lost his home to foreclosure shortly after being appointed the Treasury Secretary of the United States. He was in charge of the financial standing of the United States, yet he was unable to manage his own finances effectively. I don't say that to highlight any deficiencies in our former Treasury Secretary, but to demonstrate that intelligence does not negate the shortcomings of humanity.

There were only a few times when Jesus warned His disciples, but His words, "Take heed how you hear" (Luke 8:18), forever ring in my mind. We must be cognizant of our frailty as humans and humbled by it. If we are mindful of the errors in the code that has been programmed into our thinking over our years of existence, it will help us make healthy financial decisions and free us to follow the purpose God has outlined in our spirits.

Here I will deal with the psychology of money, known as behavioral finance, and many of the psychological traps we find ourselves in. In this school of psychology, there have been many discoveries around the biases we as humans often succumb to. They are like a bear trap hidden artfully under the brush of everyday life in our subconscious. My goal is to show you the signs to look for so that you don't keep falling into the same trap. If you are aware of them, then you will have more power to overcome them. Jesus said, "The truth will set you free."

I encourage you to explore these concepts with me, armed with an open mind. God has given you resources, time, energy, and a history that, if used well, will become tools in the hands of the master craftsman. Here we will explore some of the challenges of the mind and how they affect your financial decisions. Also, having a team, micro church, and mentor will help you have a sounding board of objective voices who can assist you in avoiding these traps.

ANCHORING

As humans, we often attach reality and our outlook of future events to our most recent events. Think about a failed relationship. How often have you, or others you have cared about, struggled with the expectation that this new wonderful relationship will end in the same manner? Struggles with a past supervisor lead us to believe this new boss will one day turn into the tyrant we just left behind.

Anchoring is the epitome of being ruled by our past. Many of these psychological biases are driven by our history, which often becomes the enemy of our future if it is not addressed. In Philippians 3:13, Paul says, "But one thing I do: forgetting what lies behind and straining forward to what lies ahead...." This is the cure for anchoring and many of the other biases I will outline here.

I've seen many, many clients who are anchored to the nasty

recession and declines of the stock market between October, 2007 and March, 2009. Job loss, market declines, and fear were so heavily embedded in their minds that it has become hard to not expect it will happen again soon. As I stated earlier, recessions are a normal occurrence, no matter how bad they are. We must act proactively and prudently according to the economic season at hand, but we must not allow our fear of the past repeating itself to dictate our decisions. Anchoring will lead us down a path of overreaction and over-optimism. It will cause us to step into a world of emotion and fear instead of wisdom and truth.

The year of 1999 saw more money invested into stock mutual funds than the rest of the 1990s combined, according to the research of a large mutual fund company. Anchoring works both ways. Sometimes it can lead us to be afraid of good days ahead, while at other times we can become overly optimistic. Either occasion will end in a destructive result. We will either miss opportunities due to the fear of the past repeating itself, or we may find ourselves taking inappropriate risks with the expectation that nothing bad can happen. "Having a clear eye," as Jesus said, is the goal and the ultimate weapon against all of these biases.

Observe the past and learn the lessons it can teach you, but don't make future decisions based on an expectation that is anchored in the past. Let objectivity be a foundation to stand on when you are making financial decisions. It will provide not only a firm place to stand but also an elevated perspective, so you can see your path more clearly, without the stains of the past.

MENTAL ACCOUNTING

Mental accounting is the concept that describes why we deal with different sources of income with different perspectives. Our paychecks are used to pay bills, save, give, and enjoy a bit with what's left over. However, if we receive a large tax return or inheritance, we often will view that differently than our paycheck. This is why over 90 percent of all lottery winners who are immediate multi-millionaires end up in bankruptcy.

I've been witness on countless occasions of someone inheriting hundreds of thousands of dollars or more, only to find themselves penniless within a few years. They had fun, took trips they could never afford on their salaries, and made purchases they would soon be unable to maintain. When I find I'm meeting with a new potential client who recently received a windfall, I always ask, "Were you living paycheck-to-paycheck before?" If the answer is yes, the result will almost always be the same. Soon enough they will be right back there.

The key to overcoming the adverse affects of mental accounting is to view every dollar the same. Let's say you receive a $500,000 inheritance. How many hours, or even years in some cases, would you need to work to generate that much income? Would you throw away all of the money made over that period of time? What about a $100,000 bonus at work? How long would you work to make that bonus in your regular paycheck? Be diligent, have a plan based on your goals, and when a windfall occurs, you will have some place to catch it; otherwise, it will be cast to the wind.

CONFIRMATION AND HINDSIGHT

The past can also hold us hostage with two realities called confirmation bias and hindsight. With confirmation bias, we have the tendency to view recent events in light of our beliefs or expectations. We view events from the perspective that they are confirming what we expected to happen. This is true with investing particularly. I can't tell you how many times I have seen individuals and professionals take credit for gravity. The market goes up in certain seasons. When it does, investors are quick to take credit for their investing prowess. Often their success is really just luck or simple market dynamics, not their ability to time the market or pick the best stock. Professionals and day traders are quick to take credit for the growth of their portfolio's performance when it's good. Often, with a little analysis, you will find that they have not fared very well compared with the S&P 500 or whichever index would be appropriate. They are quick to use the current success as confirmation of their intelligence and "gut," but they downplay the lack of performance when it's not there. Arrogance is akin to confirmation bias.

Hindsight is the "knew it all along" bias. We often pretend we predicted events after they occurred. The real problem here is that we pretend we have the ability to predict the next unfolding of events. I'm not saying we can't predict future events, but we must be careful to be doing so from an educated, unbiased, and objective viewpoint.

The key with both of these biases is that they are rooted in a preconceived notion that we are blind to. The truth is, we will not always be right! And that's OK. We will be better able to make healthy decisions if we are not pinned down by the notion that we must be right all of the time. Give yourself permission to take chances but not marry yourself to that decision. Be prepared to walk away if the deal goes south. Sell the stock before you lose too much. It's OK to anticipate an outcome; however, if it turns 180 degrees against you, pull the plug.

There's only one commitment that carries a lifetime vow, and that's marriage. Don't make investment decisions with a view too far into the future. Look at the next investment into your future, whether it's a business deal, stock purchase, or something else, from the perspective of "What's most appropriate based on the information I have available?" If new information becomes available that would lead you to change that decision, it's OK to change your mind. Give yourself permission to change direction or strategies. Adapt!

I know this will be hard for many. We live in a time when the Church often blindly walks into the future without a sense of consequence. Then we look for information to support our beliefs. We look at the past and say, "That will never happen again," but we continue to repeat it. We must begin with a clean slate and make decisions with a sound mind, unclouded by the past or future. If we take care of today (see Matt. 6:34), as Jesus said, we will be far less likely to fall prey to these slave drivers.

GAMBLER'S FALLACY

Let's flip a coin. Heads or tails? Let's say we play this game 100 times. If the first ten flips land on the heads side of the coin, what would be your guess for the next flip? You see, on each coin flip, you have a 50 percent chance of being correct. What may be surprising is that even after ten results of heads being the winner, the odds of the next flip is still 50/50. Odds don't change based on the past. They remain constant according to behavioral psychologists.

We often think we will be right the next time, which is called gambler's fallacy. "The next roll of the dice will turn my way." This is the mantra of many addicts to the games. But they are wrong; the odds are stacked against them.

There's also a statistical concept known as mean reversion. The mean (average) will always draw the data back to itself when we're dealing with a large pool of numbers. This is a strategy I have used in investing successfully for many years. When an asset class moves too far in one direction outside of the historical average, it will almost always (usually triggered by a catalyst) be drawn back to the middle and maybe beyond. It's like a pendulum, back and forth.

The difference between using mean reversion versus falling victim to gambler's fallacy is distinct. Gambler's fallacy involves believing you'll be right without any evidence to support that belief. It's like the definition of insanity ascribed to Albert Einstein—continuing to do the same thing expecting a different result.

Let's say you evaluate a stock and select it based on your belief it will grow over the next twelve months, but you're wrong. It tanks and you lose a third of your investment. Would you change your evaluation process? Would you seek professional guidance and input? Would you read educational material to increase your understanding? Regretfully, most people don't. That's gambler's fallacy at work. It says, "I'm not going to change the bet I'm making, because this time it will work."

Even though I don't expect many hardcore gamblers will read this book, I feel it's important to make an observation based on my experience advising many in an effort to help them overcome this bias. Many feel their past losses are justified. Past business deals gone awry were someone else's fault. We must humbly admit when we need professional assistance. I have numerous professionals I rely on for guidance and information—some simply for utility and others to protect me from myself. I know I don't know everything. Some things I'm very good at; others, not so much.

If you want to avoid gambler's fallacy, you can. The key is to see that next decision, or coin flip if you will, for what it is. Don't interpret it based on past results. Don't be a contrarian for the sake of it. Accept the next decision based on the merits it potentially produces. Consider the influences to the outcome clearly. Don't be guided by an expectation; rather, let the details create the expectation, for better or worse.

HERD BEHAVIOR

Lemmings are cute, little, fury mole-like creatures. In their migration they will move in herds, sometimes over a cliff and into a lake to swim to the other side. They tumble like water rolling over a waterfall. They follow blindly, one after another, as if no other path is possible. Some may die in that effort, but the next keeps coming.

We often behave the same way. I can't tell you how many times someone has told me about what their friend is investing in or how their brother is doing so well, which is why they want to follow suit. Most humans don't like isolation. We all have a desire to be connected with others. Gangs are popular with young people who are on the fringe of society because they find a place they can "fit in." When I was a teen, my parents warned me about the negative power of the phrase, "Everybody's doing it." Peer pressure is effective because of this embedded emotional need.

A great example of this is your neighbor or brother-in-law who is certain you should follow in his footsteps with the most recent investment he made. He probably is not fully aware of your circumstances and may not even completely understand the transaction he just completed. Yet, he believes that if he did it, you should too. We don't like to be the only one! Whether we win or lose, most of us just don't want to be alone. That desire, which is normal and part of the beauty of God's design for the human race, will also lead us in the wrong direction if we are unaware of it.

The key to overcoming herd behavior is confidence. Doubt is a distinguisher. It determines what's possible and what's not. It causes us to look around for others who are doing something to confirm that it's OK to move forward. Doubt is a hesitation to action that will cripple us and cause us to second guess our financial decisions. Buyer's remorse is a costly endeavor, typically, both emotionally and financially. Regret hurts.

Instead, when you evaluate a decision properly and conclude the appropriate course of action, you may be alone. Do it anyway! Jump out of the boat! Cast your net! Start that business and take your first foray into new territories. Of course, you should seek the counsel of others who have had success in that area and, make sure to do your own homework, too. Don't be influenced by the herd. Rather, be conscientious, armed with wisdom and the guidance of the Holy Spirit. Most would never do what you're about to embark on.

The masses are content with insignificance and mediocrity. Don't settle for that. Others will try to hold you back with distractions and time-consuming activities. Move on! Jesus said in Luke 14:26, "If anyone comes to Me and does not hate his father and mother and wife and children and brothers and sisters, yes, and even his own life, he cannot be my disciple." If you are expected to hate—or forsake—your most loved family members, then of course you should expect to leave the herd behind. Follow His voice, and let others do what they will.

OVERCONFIDENCE EFFECT

Confidence and optimism are mandatory if you're going to excel as God intended when He created you. The unsettling truth of the matter, however, is that you must be careful not to allow overconfidence to rule the day. We often take small victories to determine that we are ready for the big time. Often, vision does not directly result in outcomes. Successfully accomplishing your mission requires much, much more.

I know many who have grand ideas but very little implementation and results. They are going to change the world one day in their minds. However, when presented with opportunities to be mentored, they shun them. Instead of taking significant action toward their prize, they live in utter distraction. It's a simple thing. Be a lifelong disciple. Find someone who is doing what you want to do with success, and then become a student. You may want to alter the techniques and create your own personal touch to your expression as you develop competence. As you learn, you may find you've been developing relevant skills all along. You just didn't know why. The Holy Spirit has been guiding you through your passions, even without your awareness.

However, the overconfidence effect is a bias that can cause our interpretation of our abilities and judgments to go well beyond the results we are currently producing. You've had some successes, and you should absolutely celebrate them. However, always keep a humble heart and be a constant disciple of Christ. God even used a donkey once, so don't think too highly of yourself.

According to bestselling author Stephen Covey, there are four stages to building competency in a skill. Unconscious incompetence is the first, in which you don't even know what you don't know. At this stage, it is often others who tell you what to do, and you, hopefully, follow their direction. Eventually things start to click, and you become consciously incompetent. Here you know that you're not very good, but with intentionality you are developing skill. The next stage is conscious competence. At this point, you have learned some of the finer points of your task and have developed a degree of skill. Focus is a big contributor at this stage. If you make a conscious effort, you can produce fantastic results, but you need to do the activities on purpose. The final stage is unconscious competence. This is the point of mastery. It's the flow of the moment, and results just happen.

It doesn't require much conscious effort for me to put a fork to my mouth. I don't give a moment's thought to signing my name. There was a point in all of our lives when these simple activities were laborious and messy. The best pitchers in Major League Baseball at one point threw a baseball for the first time and probably with very little accuracy. Of course, those same all-star baseball players, and all other highly successful athletes, have coaches.

One key to conquering the overconfidence effect is letting your results be your judge—not your interpretation of yourself. Jesus said, "Each tree is known by its own fruit" (Luke 6:44). This is often used as a direction for discernment of someone's intentions. I encourage you to take it on as a mirror of your own abilities. Just because you had success in your last decision doesn't mean you should move forward blindly. The people of Israel found themselves under the rebuke of God many times because they bought into the lie of overconfidence. That's where the holy grail of overcoming comes into play—transparency.

James 5:16 says to "confess your sins to one another." I suggest you take that spirit of transparency on in every endeavor. Connect with others who can see God's plan and purpose in your life and can walk with you in love. Seek out others who have a degree of mastery in your field that exceeds your own, and submit to them in humility. Take criticism constructively, whether it's intended that way or not. You have some skills, but don't allow overconfidence to steer you off a cliff. Be accepting of yourself and your current status. Any great endeavor begins with first acknowledging and accepting where you are right now. It's like the GPS on your phone. How good would the directions to your next destination be if it could only narrow down your current location to a 10 mile radius?

Let me be clear. Confidence is not bad. In fact, it is necessary for you to climb your mountain. You must be confident in your God-given abilities and His will to provide the wisdom and resources to accomplish the mission He has designated for you. You will be faced with moments, like David facing Goliath, when you will have to go against conventional wisdom to overcome an enemy and climb your mountain. However, I run into a lot of people who are blinded by their preconceived notions and are completely inflexible to outside feedback. They continue to make bad decisions, confident that the results will be different next time. Having an objective climbing team will provide the feedback necessary to keep you from falling off the cliff. Be open and flexible to their feedback.

OVERREACTION

As I mentioned previously, pessimism dominates our society today. Jim Morrison expressed the general outlook well: "The future is uncertain but the end is always near." This is a sad way to look at life. But for many, it is reality. I found it fascinating, during the last recession, to see how the media reacted to the falling stock prices and the downfall of companies like Bear Sterns and Lehman Brothers. It was the end of capitalism and the potential fall of the financial infrastructure of our country. Even today it holds true, as business news networks tout the remarkable increases of 100 or 200 points for the Dow Jones Industrial Average or express their deepest concerns over a 150 point decline.

Toward the end of the recession, in the spring of 2009, bond prices for high-yield "junk" bonds were priced as if approximately 75 percent of the companies who issued them were already out of business. Bank stocks were priced as if the financial industry had already collapsed, despite the government initiating the Troubled Asset Relief Program (TARP), which was instituted in the fall of 2008. TARP placed a legitimate guarantee by the federal government on the major banks in the U.S. Essentially the U.S. government would not allow them to go out of business and would support them in the event that bad investment losses put them at risk of insolvency (not having enough money to survive). However, the market kept overreacting to the fear that was present.

Most recently, at the end of August 2015, we had declines that were outside of the norm, and suddenly it was Y2K all over again. We then had blood moon Shemita-ites who were certain judgment on America was imminent and the current declines were the fulfillment of prophecy. In the eyes of some, to quote Jim Morrison, "The end is always near." Sometimes overreaction becomes a self-fulfilling prophecy, and we must guard against that. If we don't change our ways, we will drive this beautiful nation of ours into the ground.

The point is, we must be careful to be clear about what is real and what is a dramatization of reality. There are things we must address, decisions we must make. However, we should not overreact to an ant hill and create an insurmountable mountain filled with giants.

Israel was driven into a wilderness of wandering because of an overreaction to the puny giants in the promised land. The would-be apostles were rebuked by Christ for making a fuss over a little storm. Don't overreact. Rather, take a deep breath and make decisions. Calm your emotions and allow the executive center of your brain to judiciously judge a situation. Then God will be able to speak, and wisdom will come. Mountains will move, and giants will become grasshoppers right before your eyes.

AVAILABILITY BIAS

Availability bias is the tendency we have to place a higher weight on the most recent information available. Despite our past, consistent experiences, and empirical evidence, we often will unknowingly change our behavior and decision-making processes based on new information. Of course, we should use current information when making decisions, so let me explain further.

If things are good, they will only get better; if things are bad, they are bound to get worse. This applies to both investing in the capital markets as well as making personal decisions. I've seen people with illnesses blow up their finances, thinking their life was beyond their control. Others have turned career developments and an imminent raise into an opportunity to overextend their finances. Later, they discovered they couldn't afford the new lifestyle they thought was within reason.

You may find that many of these biases overlap and even cooperate at times, and you're right. Jeremiah 17:9 says, "The heart is deceitful above all things, and desperately sick; who can understand it?" For this reason, you must, "Keep your heart with all diligence, for out of it spring the issues of life" (Prov. 4:23 NKJV). All of our decisions, financial and otherwise, are made from a deep place inside our souls. If you familiarize yourself with these various mental landmines, which we all share, and watch for them as you make decisions, you will be much more likely to identify the traps the enemy of your soul has placed in your path. With a heart of humility, you are empowered with both the knowledge I have just given you and the wisdom to acknowledge where your frailty meets faith and His grace becomes sufficient.

LAYERING

Often, these various biases that we use in making financial decisions become layered, like a set of multicolored glasses. Be careful to identify what premises you are applying to your decisions, and remove them one by one. Becoming familiar with the biases will also allow you to identify them in others, guard yourself from the ill advice of others, build others up as you identify their blind spots, and even use them to take advantage of the psychological missteps in the marketplace.

On March 6, 2009, I attended a conference with several hundred advisors. The market had continued falling due to the recession, the real estate bubble bursting, and the overall calamity present in the financial markets. As I observed the environment, I was able to see how schizophrenic the markets seemed. We would get good news and the market would have a horrible day; bad news would send the market up. It just didn't seem rational.

I saw these biases in play right before my eyes, but it wasn't just an individual. It was showing itself in decisions being made in *all* of the markets. Fear was gripping the minds of investors, and I knew all they needed was a tiny ray of light to turn things around. That began to play out at the end of February, when Citigroup announced they were profitable so far for the year. On March 6, Bank of America then announced the exact same thing. These were two of the worst hit financial firms, and they were suddenly running positive revenues after consistently writing off tens of millions of dollars of bad debt over the last few quarters. I knew this was significant.

After catching this news during a break in the conference, I went back and told my buddies, who were fellow attendees, that this would signify the bottom of the market. They all laughed at me, but I was right. The following Monday, March 9, was the bottom, and the market shot up 57 percent that summer. I made some bets that financial stocks would turn positive quickly, and I saw options contracts I purchased double in one day and continue to move up from there. A lot of money can be made if you can identify how the biased behavior of others can be capitalized on, and I just gave you the tools to do it in every marketplace.

DECLARATION

I have a renewed mind, and I am not bound to relive my past (see Rom. 12:2).

MOUNTAIN CLIMBING STEPS

42. Of the mental biases, which two are you most prone to giving in to?

43. What steps will you take to ensure you are clearheaded when making financial decisions?

44. Pray five minutes per day for the next 21 days for a clear mind and pure heart when making financial decisions. Be specific regarding decisions you must make in the near future.

CHAPTER 13

PERCEIVE THE SEASON; THINK STRATEGICALLY

In chapter 9, I asked you to imagine what it would be like to be a farmer reaping your hard-earned harvest. You prepared your field, planted your seeds, and tended the crops as they grew. When you reap them, you discover you have achieved a stellar crop. This is due, in large part, to your many years of farming experience and the accompanying skills that you've developed. However, now you are facing the fact that you are growing older and cannot move as fast as you once did. In light of this, you ask yourself some questions. Do you halt your endeavors since you have amassed a self-sustainable wealth? Do you give in to the realization that you may not desire to continue to work? Is it too hard now to continue your pursuits? Perhaps you should just change your perspective.

Earlier, I suggested that investment and overall financial decisions should be evaluated according to the economic climate or season. Another concept that must be considered in the decision-making process is the season of life you are currently walking in. Self-awareness is a cornerstone of emotional intelligence, and in my experience, it is a key to overall success in decision-making. We often find it difficult to be transparent with others. Our degree of transparency will never exceed the trust we have for the other party. For this reason, transparency with ourselves is often not only challenging, but also one of the most difficult tasks we embark upon.

Being honest with ourselves requires we forgive ourselves for our past mistakes. First, we must be honest about mistakes and accept what is sometimes a gruesome truth. We have all lied, had hatred in our hearts, betrayed, wasted, behaved in an untrustworthy manner, and so on. Paul went so far in First Timothy 1:15 to say "that Christ Jesus came into the world to save sinners, of whom I am chief" (NKJV). He owned the reality of the destruction that he had levied upon the believers of Christ. This honesty with himself allowed him (I believe) to embrace the reality he proclaimed two verses later—"Now to the King eternal, immortal, invisible, to God who alone is wise, be honor and glory forever and ever. Amen" (1 Tim. 1:17 NKJV).

In the same way, we must forsake the false humility that often leads to hubris and self-righteousness, and we must embrace the reality of our forgiven and redeemed mistakes. This will then unlock a new reality in Christ's glory for our lives. We then can see the future and face financial decisions from a new perspective, embracing the wisdom we have learned from our past and additional research. This, combined with the leadership of the Holy Spirit, will cause us to face decisions from a mountain top perspective and move forward with boldness.

David asked a question in Psalm 24:3, "Who may ascend into the hill of the LORD? Or who may stand in His holy place?" (NKJV). In the following verse, he answers:

> He who has clean hands and a pure heart, who has not lifted up his soul to an idol, nor sworn deceitfully. He shall receive blessing from the Lord, and righteousness from the God of his salvation (Psalm 24:4–5 NKJV).

We must prayerfully consider the motivations that drive us to action. We must also confront the lies that have held us in the prison of inaction. In this we will find the generous acceptance of grace that will empower us to climb with boldness and passion. With a heart full of commitment to His Kingdom and glory, we will find a renewed perspective and freedom from the restrictions that have held us.

Let me be clear, we must forsake the past—both the good and the bad. It's important to celebrate our past victories and to view our mistakes as the learning experiences they are. We must, however, begin each new day as a blank sheet of paper. Each new day gives us an opportunity to create upon the picture that God placed in our hearts when He breathed life into us.

In this process, there will be times when you must jump out of a boat, like Peter, when the opportunity does not seem ideal. Be sure you have clear eyes and ears so that you can hear the master's voice distinctly. Peter said to Jesus, "If it's you, call me." He wanted to be sure about who was calling him to step onto the raging waters. Then, Jesus called him by name.

Many times, however, you will be faced with decisions that require wisdom and sound judgment. Timing is everything. Boldly moving into a new market requires identifying the door as it opens so that you get there first. Watch and pray as you do this. You can avoid a lot of trouble by having a climbing team with you on your journey. The journey will be full of dangerous caverns you must traverse, so do it with all senses engaged and with a trusted mentor to help you avoid falling to your demise.

Having access to money is also critical as you make these steps, so be certain to know the cost of an endeavor and the availability of resources prior to jumping. Don't start climbing a rock face if you're not certain you have enough rope to make it.

DECLARATION

I have the understanding of Issachar, perceiving the times and seasons, because I am one with the one who knows all.

MOUNTAIN CLIMBING STEPS

45. In 50 words or less, describe the current season of life you are in.

46. What actions are you being compelled to take in this season that are not your normal routine?

47. What activities should you discontinue based on the season you are currently in?

CHAPTER 14

CLIMBING MOUNTAINS

Climbing a mountain is not easy. As the old saying goes, "If it was easy, everyone would be doing it." Mount Everest is the highest peak on earth at over 29,000 feet elevation. It requires years and tens of thousands of dollars spent on training and equipment to attempt to reach the summit of this formidable foe. Climbing a mountain is not a task to be taken lightly either. The skills and equipment needed require intense planning and detailed preparation. Not only is reaching this peak an arduous task, but it also involves understanding the risks of rapidly changing weather patterns, which have sent many to their demise. Climber's minds and bodies must also have the opportunity to adapt to changes in the oxygen level of the air as they traverse this behemoth. Without that, they have foolishly chosen a destructive path.

Likewise, in Luke 14 Jesus gave several examples of why preparation is important for success. He talked about a builder attempting an aggressive endeavor, saying that he should first ensure his success before beginning the work. He also discussed the importance of a king considering battle with an adversary. That king would be a fool if he did not evaluate the armies and resources of his foe prior to engaging in battle. Actually it would be better to negotiate terms by way of delegates prior to engaging in battle if he was not confident that his strength was greater than that of his enemy. Jesus used these parables as a picture of discipleship.

If you've read this far in this book, you are feeling a drawing on your life, which is the will of Heaven burning deep inside. You may not be able to fully articulate it, but it's there. You may be a prisoner to your current career, just as Joseph was. You may have run from an enemy, or you may be wandering in the wilderness, just close enough to see your promise in the distance but not feeling empowered to enter the gates. I've been there.

I know betrayal, pain, abuse, chains, and all sorts of disappointment. Often these resulted from my own mistakes or bad timing. At times, it was others' activities or failure to seek to understand the circumstances that brought me into the lion's dens. However, as with many of you, I can say today that God was with me and has brought me to this most remarkable hour in history. I found a content dissatisfaction that kept me going. A fire and will burned in my heart; I knew God had chosen me, which was confirmed by numerous prophets and mentors.

I am not alone. God is raising up mountain climbers! A vision has been unfolding for a couple of decades now; it is beginning to take shape. God is looking for willing participants, those who see discipleship as more than simply living a good, loving, and moral life. Rather, they are on a mission. They have an intensity to their desires that not everyone shares. They speak a language that is not common at Sunday morning services in America today. They see the world differently.

In Exodus 32:17, we find Joshua and Moses descending the mountain where they met God. The nation of Israel had grown weary of the absence of their leader and decided to devise their own god to worship. Joshua came within earshot of the party taking place below, and his initial response speaks volumes: "There is a noise of war in the camp." This initial perception was quickly corrected, as he was able to distinguish singing. But initially, he had heard war.

Many in the Church today are celebrating the small victories and praying for past revivals and manifestations to resume. However, I believe God has an alternate agenda. God does not want to move into a church building and bring His glorious manifestation there. He wants to take the pulpits into the streets and marketplaces of the cities of the world. He wants to raise up those who will climb the mountain of the Lord in private and then climb the mountains of the world in the public eye.

Politicians, business people, educators, artists, athletes, and so on are being selected for a move of God that will alter the face of culture over the next twenty years. They will place a stake in the ground on the throat of the enemy of our souls and begin to demonstrate that all of God's enemies are His footstool. That demonstration is not about just a prayer, but rather about having skills and support in place to maintain momentum while avoiding chasms of death and destruction along the way.

No one climbs a major mountain alone. There is always a team of like-minded and trained members who have diverse backgrounds and skill sets but share a singular focus on the summit. Build your team. Jesus prayed for us in John 17:21, "That they all may be one, as You, Father, are in Me, and I in You; that they also may be one in Us, that the world may believe that You sent Me" (NKJV). I perceive a growing need for unity in the body of mountain climbing believers. You need to work with a team of individuals who are all trying to climb your mountain. There are many paths and peaks on any given mountain, so let go of any jealousy or selfishness. Serve others, and allow yourself to be served on your journey. Your team should not consist of friends who are all at the same place as you. There should be some who are farther up the mountain than you and others who may not be as strong as you. Learn to follow and lead.

The skills you are building are not about just praying or being a good person. Jesus was not all that nice to the money changers who defiled the Temple (see Matt. 21:12). Was He acting in love when He overturned their tables and chased them out with a whip? Of course He was, but His mission was beyond being liked or respected by all. There will be those who don't appreciate, respect, or even agree with what you're about to accomplish. That's where your climbing team comes in. Don't waste time with doubters or those who hold you back. Love them, but keep moving. Your climbing Sherpa, or guide, will be a great resource in that process. You will also find renewed passion from watching the development of those who follow you. Your mission is great, so grab some hands and climb.

It's not about achieving social or economic status in the Kingdom of Heaven. The summit is the fulfillment of the mission of Heaven for our generation. We need master climbers to lead the way and others around us to provide support, information, insight, and guidance to keep us moving up the mountain. Building your own climbing team is critical to your success.

The tools I have outlined in this book provide a foundation of building blocks that apply to every mountain or sphere of influence you will endeavor to invade. The perspectives, revelation, and information shared here comes from several decades of research. I have spent tens of thousands of dollars, read hundreds of books, and prayed hours upon hours over what I have shared with you here. This is simply a foundation, though; you have much to pursue and understand regarding your specific mountain. Now, go and be the next city on a hill in your field.

DECLARATION

I am about my Father's business and am more than capable of climbing this mountain, bringing the Kingdom of Heaven to earth
(see Num. 13:30).

MOUNTAIN CLIMBING STEPS

48. List at least three people you currently know and want on your mountain climbing team.

49. Speak to those three people about your mountain climbing mission. Ask them to challenge you and support you on your climb.

50. Commit to taking radical action on your climb.